Because You Loved Me and Never Let Go

Because You Loved Me and Never Let Go

*A Fathers love
for his daughter*

Shamara Rainforest

TATE PUBLISHING
AND ENTERPRISES, LLC

This book is designed to provide accurate and authoritative information with regard to the subject matter covered. This information is given with the understanding that neither the author nor Tate Publishing, LLC is engaged in rendering legal, professional advice. Since the details of your situation are fact dependent, you should additionally seek the services of a competent professional.

The opinions expressed by the author are not necessarily those of Tate Publishing, LLC.

Published by Tate Publishing & Enterprises, LLC
127 E. Trade Center Terrace | Mustang, Oklahoma 73064 USA
1.888.361.9473 | www.tatepublishing.com

Tate Publishing is committed to excellence in the publishing industry. The company reflects the philosophy established by the founders, based on Psalm 68:11,
"The Lord gave the word and great was the company of those who published it."

Book design copyright © 2016 by Tate Publishing, LLC. All rights reserved.
Cover design by Norlan Balazo
Interior design by Shieldon Alcasid

Published in the United States of America

ISBN: 978-1-68333-351-7
Family & Relationships / Parenting / Single Parent
16.04.14

Acknowledgments

FIRST, I'D LIKE to thank my Father God, Savior and Holy Spirit. I pray this book will reap a harvest for His kingdom as He receives all the glory, honor, and praise that are due Him. I am nothing without you Lord. I live for you my El Shaddai, Jehovah-Jireh, and Jehovah-Rapha.

I must also thank all the people who have played a role in nudging me toward the Lord, and I humbly ask forgiveness of the many souls I wounded along my journey to Him. Whether I hurt you in word or deed, by my conduct, or by compromising my values, I am so sorry.

I would like to say thank you, Dad, for serving your country, loving your children, and dying daily to serve the Father. I pray you see the harvest of your seeds planted in eternity. Your encouragement and smile are more precious than silver, and I love you.

A special thank-you to my stepmother, for not giving up on my dad, you truly have not compromised your walk with the Father.

Special gratitude goes to my mother. She helped me, believed in me, and understood my purpose in writing "for our Father." (Mom, it's not what you didn't do that matters. When I think of you, I remember all the good you have done and the love you have poured out on so many since you put your faith in Jesus, our Redeemer. I love you!)

Much love and appreciation also belong to all my children who suffered so many hardships and abuse due to my poor choices and difficult situations. I may have failed your expectations several times as your mother. (Always remember not to doubt the Father because He himself said, "I will not in any way fail you, nor give you up nor leave you without support. I will not in any degree leave you helpless nor forsake you or let you down nor relax my hold on you!" We will all fail Him, but He forgives. I ask for your forgiveness).

And to my precious daughters-in-law's. I am so thankful for your help and encouragement. Thank you for being strong and faithful to my sons and giving me my precious and beautiful grandchildren, who give me so much to live for.

And finally, thank you, Bethany, for all your hard work and willingness to complete the journey with me. I could not have done this without you, my friend and cowriter/editor.

I would also like to thank the real-life members of all the foster families portrayed in this book for taking me into your home and accepting me as one of their own. I recognize that their memories of the events described in this book are different from my own. Each of you are fine, decent, hardworking, and honest people.

This book was not intended to hurt any family members, relatives, friends, congregations of any church, or pastors. Both my publisher and I regret any unintentional harm resulting from the publishing and marketing of *Because You Loved Me and Never Let Go*. I have gone to great lengths to see that the names and setting are different.

I understand that our lives change in the course of time, and we have a loving and forgiving God. I have forgiven anyone who has brought harm to my children or me. I also would ask that you forgive me and understand that I made some poor choices.

I have mentioned acts of abuse, violence, and mention of drugs and using of drugs. As I have said, my intent is not to *expose* your privacy of matters of our past that you have wished to remain quiet about.

My intentions are merely to help someone who may be in similar situations to identify the characteristics and understand that consequences may bring our loved ones and us a lifetime of pain and regret.

My intent is only to show that "love covers a multitude of sins."

God is Love, and He has said, "He who has not ever sinned throw the first stone, then neither do I condemn you, go and sin no more your sins are forgiven." We all have made mistakes we would like to forget, and God forgives and forgets, so I pray that if you have not made Jesus your Lord yet, then you will consider doing so.

Lastly, I will point out that due to my identity being unknown except to close friends and immediate family members, no one but yourself could possibly know who your character name is. My children and immediate family have known all the incidences mentioned because they were involved.

Anyone who reads the book I pray would keep the characters' identities unknown for their protection, as well as all of ours. We all have a past, and it's not God's will that anyone slander anybody, so please be understanding to their privacy.

Thank you,
Shamara

Contents

Preface

To THE MANY who feel insignificant and abandoned, abused, and rejected, without purpose and without a home. The Father is waiting to help you. To forgive you. To provide spiritual blessings that exceed anything you could imagine. May He show you His plan for *your* life.

I pray you will learn to lean on Him and trust Him when the battle seems more than you can handle.

"The Lord is good, A stronghold in the day of trouble; And He knows those who trust in Him" (Nah. 1:7).

"Jesus said to him, 'You shall love the Lord your God with all your heart, with all your soul, and with all your mind'" (Matt. 22:37).

"Heaven and earth will pass away, but My words will by no means pass away" (Matt. 24:35).

People change, laws change, and generations change, but rest assured God does not change and neither does His Word. Come follow Him, and His ways lead to everlasting life in His kingdom. Many will lead you to believe lies and tell you that certain things are okay to do, and the government passes laws that says you can do these things, but God is Truth: "He is the same yesterday, today, and forever." Walk His way and you will not be lead astray!

Many roads and many sources giving you directions can lead you down the wrong paths. (Remember, God didn't put you there, and you will have to suffer consequences. God does work all things out for good [Rom. 8:28].) The Father gave us directions to let us know where we are, where we are going, and where we need to be. It is never too late to make a U-turn and recalculate.

"Never give up. Just let go and let God."

"It is better to be safe than sorry."

"If in doubt, don't."

"Be broken, be free."

"Love is blind, but the neighbors aren't."

"Those whom live in glass houses shouldn't throw stones."

> O Lord, You have searched me and known me. You know my sitting down and my rising up; You understand my thought afar off. You comprehend my path and my lying down, And are acquainted with all my ways. For there is not a word on my

tongue, But behold, O Lord, You know it altogether. You have hedged me behind and before, And laid Your hand upon me. (Ps. 139:1–5)

Introduction

> God sent forth His Son, born of a woman, born
> under the law, to redeem those who were under the
> law, that we might receive the adoption as sons...
> Therefore you are no longer a slave but a son, and
> if a son, then an heir of God through Christ.
>
> —Galatians 4:4–5, 7

IN LUKE 15, the Bible tells of a son who demands that his father give him his inheritance early. The youth spends the money on partying, women, and wild living—hardly paying any attention to his quickly depleting resources. He gives no thought to what his actions cost his grieving dad, and he doesn't care. But then one day, the money runs out.

His so-called friends abandon him, and the man is left with nothing to eat but the slops of pigs. It doesn't take the young man long to realize he'd be better off as a servant in his dad's house. Although he expects to find rejection and to hear "I told you so" before he gets sent to the fields, he swallows his pride and heads home.

What he doesn't know is that his dad has been searching the horizon for him every day since his departure. When the father sees his wayward son, he runs to him, kisses him, and declares that his boy who was lost has been found. He orders a feast and places his own ring on the young man's hand. Though the son expected rejection, scolding, or outright punishment, he found mercy, grace, and love. I begin with this story because I know many people hesitate to come to God—who, by the way, is represented by the father in the parable—because they think, *I'm not good enough to talk to Him. I'm too bad. I've made too many mistakes. He won't want me!* Maybe they've spent years of their lives hearing, "You are trash. You are stupid. Nobody wants you!" But the truth is that God is full of love and compassion for His children.

He knows our struggles. He sees our dirt. He loves us anyway. A popular worship song reminds us that "God's love never fails. It never gives up. It never runs out on [us]." In fact, no matter what we've done and no matter what has been done to us, God says, "I love you. All that is mine is yours. Ask for Me, and I will come to you. I can make you clean. New." God is our Holy Heavenly Father. But the Bible says, "All have sinned and fall short of the glory of God" (Rom. 3:23).

That, of course, is a problem because we can't have a relationship with our Creator until the sin problem is dealt with, and we can't go to heaven unless we find God's forgiveness. So what do we do? Sit in the pigpen—or seek out the Father's plan for our redemption?

Imagine that a thief is found guilty and sentenced to life in prison. A rich man steps into the courtroom and says, "I will pay for this man's release. He is welcome to live in my palace, to work in my office, and to have access to everything I own. All he must do is accept my gift." This is a picture of what God does for every person who accepts His love. God's Son, Jesus Christ, died on a cross as a sacrifice for our sins. (See John 3:16.) Father God paid our sin debt with His Son's blood.

When we accept his love and forgiveness, He adopts us as His own, gives us the Holy Spirit, and promises us eternity in heaven. It's as if the God of the universe runs to us, throws His arms around our necks, and welcomes us to His home. Romans 8:15 says that when we come to Jesus for salvation, God allows us to cry out to Him as "Abba" (Aramaic for *daddy*).

Loving parents do their best to teach their children how to live in safe and constructive ways that are for their best. We say, "Don't cross that busy street alone." "Don't watch that stuff on TV." "You can't play with those toys or listen to that music." "Young man, you are *going* to church." It is a parent's job to say, "Honey, no! That is poison. Don't eat that and don't touch that." We warn them against things that can bring them harm.

One day when I was dealing with my own children, I felt God the Father speak to my heart: "Shamara, I love you the way you love your children. The way you are concerned about your child? I get concerned about you even more!"

"Father," I prayed, "they are not listening to me. Lord, I am so disappointed in their actions and their attitudes!"

He replied, "I have been disappointed with My children many times." My journey to Christ was not neat and pretty. The story of how I came to walk in daily obedience to my Father is even less so. But my life is a testimony to the fact that the Father loves His children and gives them a book full of guidance on how to live. Though He allows the natural consequences of our sin and choices to mark our lives, He always acts out of love. Everything He does is meant to draw us closer to Him, to encourage us to lean on Him more, and to make us better—stronger.

Some of us spend a lifetime trying to know what "love" really is. We look to our earthly parents, to friends, to money, to relationships, or to religion. We grieve hard when those who are supposed to be there for us fail to love us unconditionally. It hurts when they do not protect us, care for us, or approach us with the gentleness, kindness, understanding, and compassion we crave. The reality is that only God the Father can meet all our needs.

My heart has been broken. My relationships have been broken. My health has been broken. I have felt alone and dejected in a world that cursed me and abused me and judged me. I've been discouraged, rejected, and deceived. People have treated me like an outcast. And if I'm honest, I recognize that in many cases, I have reaped what I have sown.

But as I learn to put my trust in the Father, I find He comforts me, wipes my tears, heals me, provides for me, and shelters me. It's just what He does for each of His kids.

The Lord says, "Come as you are." To the poor, uneducated, rejected, abused, imprisoned, unwanted, homeless, dirty, drunken, and addicted, He says, "Come to Me…and I will give you rest" (Matt. 11:28).

This is the story of how I came to know the Father.

Jesus came not to fill us with religion but to fill us with His righteousness so He could have a personal relationship with us.

1

I Am Yours

For You formed my inward parts; You covered me
in my mother's womb. I will praise You, for I am
fearfully and wonderfully made; Marvelous are
Your works, And that my soul knows very well. My
frame was not hidden from You, When I was made
in secret, And skillfully wrought in the lowest parts
of the earth. Your eyes saw my substance, being yet
unformed. And in Your book they all were written,
The days fashioned for me, When as yet there were
none of them.

—Psalm 139:13–16

I LIKE TO think about the love and work God put
into creating me. Each person is a designer's original,
handcrafted by the Creator of the universe. When I think
about the moments leading up to my delivery, I can imagine
the Father speaking to me just before I left my mother's

womb. "My child," I hear Him whisper, "it is about time for you to be born."

"But, Father," I answer, "I don't want to leave yet. I want to stay here with You!"

In a voice full of compassion, He calmly replies, "My child, seek Me and I will be found." His voice fades as the angels begin to sing me a lullaby. My Heavenly Father, who is the King of kings, the Lord of lords, and the Great I Am, slowly lets go of my tiny hand.

Another voice, louder this time, interrupts, "The baby is breech!" A doctor grabs me to turn me around. I still emerge from the womb backward, screaming in terror, already missing the comfort of my Father's felt presence. I have spent a lifetime doing things backward and choosing the hard way, this may be why.

Moments later, I look into the eyes of my mother, Rose, who has carried me for nine months as my Father formed and loved me. She will be the one to feed me, hold me, and keep me safe as my guardian angel hovers nearby. I fall asleep, trusting that one day my Father will show me the way back home.

In coming years, however, I'll learn just how much I'll need His intervention in my life because the one holding me in her arms will prove a terrible guide.

As I share the story of my life, grace must be extended to those who will show up in my biography. Those who are serving the Lord have been forgiven by the same Father who so lovingly created me, and even those who have not accepted Him have my forgiveness. While passing judgment is easy, we do well to remember that each of us has favorite sins and shortcomings. Only with the Holy Spirit's intervention do we have any hope of overcoming our downfalls.

My mother was photogenic, easily pulling off the famous movie-star look. She was five feet nine inches tall with a slender figure and a head full of beautiful, naturally curly dark-brown hair that cascaded down her back. Rose has always been a clever, witty, desirous, flirtatious, and tenacious woman. In those days, however, she was also obnoxious, sarcastic, loud, loose, ungoverned, vulnerable, judgmental, critical, and overly opinionated. Many people would take one look at her deep-green eyes and curvy figure and decide she was beautiful on the outside. On the inside, however, she was marked by deeply embedded pain that began in her childhood.

My mom's mother had always favored her own two younger daughters, who each had a different dad. Mom didn't have a good relationship with her father either. In fact, both sets of my grandparents were abusive to my biological parents. Mom and Dad—who were never married—were reared in broken homes and saw plenty of violence, hate, and unforgiveness.

If that weren't bad enough, both were brought up under the teachings of the Mormon religion, which claims to be true yet is based on pointless tradition and lies. Mormonism's founder, Joseph Smith, created fables and false doctrines that twist the teachings of God's true Word, the Bible. Followers of his cult are left with a belief system that is empty and false. Neither Mom nor Dad knew of the Bible's words: "If any of you lacks wisdom, let him ask of God" (James 1:5). They tried to flounder through life on their own, often making a mess of things.

By the time I made my appearance in 1964, Mom had been in several relationships with the wrong type of men. She had birthed two girls before me, and we each had different fathers. She was hurting, rejected, and young. She had learned to stand up for herself because no one else would, but all the bumps in Mom's life road, coupled with her poor choices, had led her to a dark valley of pain, addictions, and suicidal attempts. She was wounded not only physically but also emotionally and mentally. All this led to multiple nervous breakdowns and a few stays in a mental hospital. My mother didn't love herself, so perhaps she couldn't demonstrate love to her children.

Mom struggled with alcohol, smoking, drugs, and a desire for men. She did not understand how to communicate with her children, and she was very harsh and physically and verbally abusive. While she did go to the Mormon church and accepted their contributions of practical provisions like food, clothing, and assistance with the bills, she had no idea that her loving Heavenly Father was willing to forgive her and to help her if only she'd come to Him through His Son. Rather than pointing her to the Gospel of Christ, the cult bogged her down with religion. Over time, she developed a mental illness and eventually went on mental disability. She also lost us [her first four girls] and was denied contact with three of them.

When I was four years old, my redheaded eldest sister, Vanessa May, went to live with my grandma. Blond-haired Scarlet Virginia, who was only a year older than me, was adopted along with my baby sister, Raylene Dawn. I was placed into a temporary foster home while Raylene's foster parents considered adopting me. When my dad, Clement, heard this, he worked to get custody of me. As soon as he could make arrangements, he took me to California to meet his wife. I stayed with her until he was out of the navy. Her name was Katie; she and their baby boy, my half brother, were living with her parents.

Katie became the only real mother I had ever known—I had largely forgotten my natural mother by the time I moved in with her. She was a genuine, candid, tenderhearted person who had a gentle spirit about her. She helped me celebrate my fifth birthday in California. Katie was my only parent until Dad came home. Anytime she had to scold me or send me to my room, she would follow up with a little talk before hugging me and telling me she loved me. I had never heard those words before.

Dad returned to us with an Australian doll he'd bought for me during his time overseas. In my eyes, my dad was my protector and provider. I believed everything he said without questioning his honesty. I was too young to realize Dad had anger and drinking problems. He adored Katie yet failed to see that he couldn't give her what she needed most.

Their relationship began to fall apart when we moved back to Ute. We lived in a small white house in Holland City. The unfinished basement was cold and dark, which was a bit frightening for a five-year-old to sleep in. I had my sixth birthday there, along with the best memories of all time.

The clowning around with Dad that ended with me getting a broken arm. Mitch being two had to have stitches after hitting his head on an end table. (He had been fetching a ball he and I were playing with.) I had recurring nightmares of a man named "Charles" coming and beating me with a belt. My dad had told me who he was and that he beat the bad man up and chased him out of town. My dad was my hero. (I later learn that he was my natural mother's ex whom I called Meany man. Apparently he had been very abusive to us girls.)

When Tonya was born, I was still six years old, and that was the last time I saw her or Mitch. I came home from school and called out for her, but she had left, taking my two half siblings with her. (By this time, I'd gained a new little sister.) I blinked my eyes behind the dorky glasses I'd recently been forced to start wearing, and I could feel the tears fall. I could not understand why Katie left—I just knew it hurt to lose her. She had neither said good-bye nor explained why she had to leave me behind. For the first time in my life, I truly felt abandoned.

Frightened, I watched Dad pack our things from that house in Templeville. My fondest memories were in that house: that was the only family I'd ever really known. I am almost sure I saw his eyes shine with moisture as he wondered how he would take care of me, let go of Katie, and get on his feet and on the right path.

I had attended a Mormon church the whole time we lived with Katie; Dad continued to drop me off at one each week, even after Katie left. In fact, I was introduced to Jesus Christ in this Mormon church. Only six years old and still stinging from Katie's absence, I would sit alone in a pew and stare up at a picture of Christ on the wall in front of me. He was kneeling in a garden, as if He were praying hard over something. This had become my favorite picture of Jesus. I vaguely realized He had some connection to God the Father. Still, I had no real grasp of Christ's importance. That would not come until much later.

Meanwhile, Dad left me with the neighbors, Mr. and Mrs. Blackenship, while he worked to get his life straightened out. This was taking longer than he anticipated, and child services became involved. The people who kept me during this season were nice enough, but the man of the house was a chiropractor. He seemed to find pleasure in adjusting my spine, and I absolutely hated it when he popped my neck.

I celebrated my seventh birthday at this neighbor's home. Before blowing out the candles, I wished for a baby sister. In retrospect, I probably just wanted Katie to come back with the baby sister she'd removed from my life.

By 1972, Dad had still not managed to settle down, and child services placed me in a foster home. This family's last name was Wills, and they had six boys. Their entire lives were built on LDS (Latter-Day Saints) principles and the Book of Mormon, which is supposed to be a follow-up revelation to the Holy Bible. (It is no such thing. Only the Bible qualifies as God's revealed Word.) Anyway, we had family home evening every Monday. On Fridays, the parents of the house went to the Mormon Temple. And every year, we faithfully watched the Mormon conference on television.

I turned eight during my time with the Wills and was confirmed and baptized as a Mormon. The confirmation and baptism didn't mean anything to me—I was more interested in celebrating at the pancake house.

Though the teachings I encountered in childhood were often off base from scriptural truth, the Lord did bring some good from them. What most stands out in my mind is a little song we kids were taught:

> I am a child of God,
> and he has sent me here
> has given me an earthly home
> with parents kind and dear
> Teach me, guide me

walk beside me
help me find the way
teach me all that I must do
to live with you some day

Something about the song became my heart's cry to the Father every time I sang it in church. Tears would roll down my face as I belted out the part about "parents kind and dear." I held on to those words with everything I had, wanting nothing more than an earthly parent's kindness, a "forever family," and a home to call my own. I so wanted God to walk by my side, teach me, guide me, and help me find the way home to Him.

One day as I was walking home from church through the park, I pondered what little I knew of God and heaven. Both topics were routinely crowded out of our religious lessons in favor of talk about Joseph Smith and Brigham Young. I knew Joseph Smith had supposedly encountered a vision of some heavenly beings who told him LDS is the only true church. Even in my youth, I realized a lot hinged on whether that was true.

"God," I asked, "if You showed this guy what the true church is, will You please tell me too?" As I think about that day, I wonder whether I subconsciously remembered the Father once telling me if I would seek Him, He would be found. I so desperately wanted my Father, but I could not reach Him through the Mormon religion: I needed Jesus (see John 14:6). While I'd seen pictures of Him, I had no idea who He really is or what He had done for me.

As 1972 rolled into 1973, my dad remarried. The woman's name was Bernice, and she had a baby girl named Cinder. That baby was my prayer answered—I loved her so much. Excited about the possibilities of my future, I moved out of the Wills's house and into a family nightmare.

From the time I was eight to shortly before my tenth birthday, my new stepmother routinely abused me. She beat me as I stood on my bed because I'd not cleaned the dishes properly. She would come at me while I was in the bathtub, scrubbing my skin raw with a copper bristle floor brush. As my poor skin bled, she'd hold my head under cold water to rinse my hair. I remember thinking, *I can't breathe! She's going to kill me!*

The abuse was psychological as well. She would cut my hair and tell me I didn't deserve long hair because I didn't take care of it. Then she would hit me with the comb and tell me I was ugly, lazy, and had the brains of a soda cracker.

On one occasion, Bernice sent me looking for a pink dress she had misplaced. When I couldn't find the dress, she beat me with a willow switch and made me pull weeds and dandelions. Another time, she tore the arms, legs, and head off my baby-doll and put the parts in a bag on my bed. She even ripped the pages out of my children's bible and threw it behind the heater. Soon after, she hissed that I had a pig nose and threw me down on a mattress clothed in nothing but a cloth diaper. "If you're going to act like a baby, you're going to get treated like one," she railed.

I was terrified of Bernice, so I tried to keep her appeased. She repeatedly woke me up at four in the morning after my dad left for work and made me wash every dish in the cabinets. Then she'd force me to stand naked on my bed while she beat me with a belt. After each instance, she warned, "Don't say anything to your dad or I will do it again tomorrow—worse." I felt so hated. I couldn't please her.

In the evenings, when Dad was home from his job at the turkey farm, things were better. He used to can pickled eggs, which I loved. When he worked at Hostess, he would bring us delicious powdered donuts with raspberry filling. Sometimes he'd even play his favorite games, Monopoly and Chinese checkers, with me.

The next morning, however, the abuse would always start over again. I would think about Dad and wonder why he couldn't see what Bernice was doing to me. Why wouldn't he stand up for me in those moments when she mistreated me in front of him? I desperately wanted my dad to protect me and stop the abuse, but he was so lost in his own issues that he seemed unable to help me with mine. I felt so unloved.

One morning, I woke up with a sore side. A spring had popped in my mattress and poked me throughout the night. I was afraid to tell my dad and stepmom about it, but I didn't think I could take another restless night on top of the ongoing abuse. I decided it was time to run away.

I spent my eleventh birthday in another shelter home and began a new ride on the foster home rollercoaster. I was in the fourth grade, and I began to ditch school. Worse, I ended up in a psychiatric ward. I got angry at a girl in my class there and dug my fingernails into her arm. When the wound became infected, her parents intervened. After that, I was officially stuck in the ward for three months. This was followed by a string of foster experiences, which included molestation and more frequent nightmares.

When I was twelve, I asked the state to return me to the Wills's foster home. And though I wasn't sure He was listening, I asked God to lead me to my natural mother. I told myself that finding my real mom would end all the drama.

2

The Tough Teen Years

The carnal mind is enmity against God; for it is
not subject to the law of God, nor indeed can be.
So then, those who are in the flesh cannot please
God.

—Romans 8:7–8

I REMEMBER 1976 and 1977 were tumultuous years for me.
Besides the issues I mentioned, I discovered pornography,
killed my hamster, and watched Dad divorce Bernice in
favor of a new stepmom: Patty. I didn't care too much for
her or for the stepbrothers and stepsister who came with
her. Still, she was an improvement.

I dreaded seventh grade because I was teased for being
a dork. Mrs. Wills made my clothes by hand; therefore, I
dreaded being seen in them. My two friends, Tonya and Kristy
(whom I had known since I was eight), played jokes on me
every chance they got. I was definitely an outcast and "nerdy."

Things got a little better when my brother, Clement Junior, was born. I loved him from the first day I laid eyes on him, but I was still in and out of various foster homes and longed for "normal." I could only see Clement Junior when I had a visiting day with Dad and Patty.

I left the Wills's (for the second time at age thirteen) house to go into another foster home, taking with me the two cats I had acquired there: Patches and Tigger. I began my monthly courses and decided it was time to stop playing with dolls and start shaving my legs.

I was done with the Mormon religion. Though I had memorized their difficult thirteen articles of faith and had been heavily immersed in their religious traditions, I decided God could not be found in the LDS church. It wasn't long before I would refuse to attend the Mormon church altogether.

In 1978, I moved in with the Porter family. They lived in a little farm house and had three daughters. One time, my foster parents took away my radio when I refused to go to their church, and I got angry. On another day, I spent the day hanging out at a friend's house and returned home later than I should have. My friend, Patrisha, was still with me, and I wanted to walk her home. Mr. Porter told me not to go. When I ignored him to walk her halfway, he chased me down, grabbed me, and threw me into the car. He took me back to the house and beat me with a board.

Before that incident, I had overdosed on NoDoz pills because I didn't want to go to school. I had hoped to go into a coma, but I ruined my own plan by filling my belly with pills meant to prevent sleep. I had to take ipecac to reverse the effects, but the treatment permanently damaged my esophagus. After that, I was put in a program for troubled teens.

I made friends at the behavioral facility where I attended group therapy and received counseling. Scotty and Patrisha were quite the pair, and Brad, who was Jewish, became my first boyfriend. He and Scotty introduced me to getting high. For the first time in my life, I felt I was among others like me; I seemed to belong. We performed puppet shows together, learned to do chores, and spent time talking openly about the baggage we carried. We were taught problem-solving skills and received help with coping with anger and communicating with our guardians. They also helped us with our homework. Yet unfortunately, all this only contributed to my growing attitude of rebellion.

My new friends and I loved to hang out at the multipurpose center where we waited for the city bus. We also attended the alternative school together and hung out in an empty storage unit where we could play spin the bottle, get high, make out, and escape from the ongoing drama of our bad home lives. Not surprisingly, going to class high did not help my academic progress, but I did get some tutoring and found that I was a speed reader. That skill translated well in helping other children learn how to read, and I soon became a tutor. I was actually good at something!

During eighth grade, Brad and I broke up. It was difficult for me to handle. I wanted to know why I was being rejected. What did I do wrong? I wondered why no one loved me. It seemed that God—if He even existed—didn't care about me either.

But then again, He did choose to answer a very specific request I had made.

Beth was a girl who hung out with our group. She was tall with curly hair and thick glasses, and she had to wear a huge back brace. In time, I would learn that her mother was related to a man who was married to my natural mother.

One day, Beth asked if she could show me something. We went to the backyard where the Porter's trailer sat and plopped down to look at some pictures. I had seen some similar photographs among my dad's things, and I knew right off my sisters and I were in the pictures Beth displayed.

Beth provided my biological mom's phone number, and I couldn't wait to go to the phone booth down the street to call her. How I wanted to hear her voice and see what she looked like! By age fourteen, I had no memory of her or of my sisters—except for Raylene Dawn, the baby. My call to Mom went something like this…

"Mom, is this you?"

"Is this Shamara?" I liked the name. I had no idea how to spell my middle name. Still, I was pleased that Beth had taken the initiative to set up a specific time to call, and my mother was expecting to hear from me.

"Yes, it's me. I usually go by Shamara. Is it okay that I'm talking with you?"

"Not until you're eighteen," she said.

I decided I didn't care. "How come you aren't allowed to see me or talk to me?"

"It's a long story."

"Well, can you tell me where my sisters are living? I still remember Raylene so well. I have these memories of us playing dress-up downstairs. We had tea parties. How old were we then?"

"You were about four. Raylene was three."

I smiled at the thought of us playing together. Though we had different fathers, Raylene and I had often been mistaken for twins. Even early on, I was the impulsive, melancholy sister, and she was energetic and chipper. After we were forced apart, some days I missed her so much I felt torn up inside.

Mom hinted that she was about to get off the phone, and I thought of another question I wanted to ask. "What is my whole name? I'm not even sure how to spell it."

She told me, explaining I'd been named after an aunt.

"Thank you," I answered, turning the information over in my mind. "I better go now. I don't want to get us in trouble."

We quickly made plans for me to visit her. I did not tell anyone I knew where she was or that we had been in touch with each other. This gave me the perfect opportunity to build up my expectations. Somehow I expected I would find a pretty, calm, loving, virtuous woman at her home near the coffin company and the scrap yard. I imagined she would be like Mrs. Cleaver on *Leave it to Beaver*, and I fully expected the woman I had dreamed about would "wow" me.

But then I saw what she was really like.

Mom was a smoker of medium build. By that time, she had short hair and wore big glasses. She never went anywhere without her movie camera and drove her big red convertible. While these details might lead some to conclude she was well situated, the truth was not so glamorous. She worked in a drycleaners and had press burn marks on her arms to prove it. It didn't take long for me to decide I didn't like my mother. She was mean, loud, and obnoxious. I found it very difficult to be around her.

Through my interactions with Mom, I met my oldest sibling, who went by Vanessa. She was living with my mother at the time—along with my half siblings, Susanna, Big Joel, and Little Joel. My mother referred to them as "hawn-yawks," her made-up word for "wicked, worthless, and stupid." She would hit them with a board or a cast-iron pan should they get out of line. Frankly, her actions sometimes paralleled Bernice's in alarming ways.

Mom was bipolar and was neurotic about the state of her floors. Though she hated dirty floors, she didn't seem bothered by a cluttered house. We had to learn to stay outside for up to three hours at a time just so she could vacuum. I also learned quickly not to sit on her furniture, not to go into her front room, and generally not to go anywhere but the kitchen. Other than that, I was only allowed in the bathroom and in the two upstairs bedrooms.

I began visiting Mom on weekends and got to know my oldest sister, Vanessa, quite well. One night, Vanessa wanted me to go to the movies with her and her friend John. He drove an old Chevy Short Bed truck. I talked my friend Scott into joining us as my date, and we went to watch *Carrie*, which I didn't like. They all started drinking, but I hated the taste of beer. I just dumped out my cans and acted like I was drunk.

After the movie, we dropped Scott off. A short time after leaving his place, something went wrong with the truck. Jim told Vanessa to steer the truck while he pushed. Because she was talking to me instead of paying attention, the truck got away from us. It rolled down the hill by itself with Vanessa and me in it and hit a pole at the bottom of the hill.

The broken windshield glass flew at us. I thought I was going to die from cuts on my head and knee. An ambulance delivered us to the hospital, and Vanessa and I both had to have stitches. The doctor called me a pansy, which I didn't appreciate. And then things got even worse when my mother made us sit in the waiting room for about five hours before she came to pick us up.

My caseworker was upset with me. In 1978, when I was in the ninth grade, she moved me to another foster home. There I met Rhonda, the housemother's biological daughter. Getting high at this particular foster home was easy to do because teenage Rhonda was also an outcast and a rebel. I liked her. She taught me how to sneak out at night, pluck my eyebrows, wear makeup, and lie about my age. She even showed me how to get my cat "high" on catnip. One night, we snuck out and went to a party where I singed my hair on a bong. I also ditched school, earned suspension, and received an all F report card.

Tammy was another friend I met during my time at this particular foster home. She schemed for us to meet up with two guys we knew and then break into some cabins where liquor was stored. At some point during this adventure, Tammy decided she wanted the guys to teach her how to drive. Now the Big Cotton Canyons are not the best place to try such a thing under normal circumstances. The fact that the guys had run out of brake fluid on top of that led to a disaster.

The jeep veered off the road and dropped off the canyon cliff! As we tumbled, I was knocked unconscious. When I woke, I was shocked to discover the vehicle had landed squarely on another dirt road. All four wheels were on the ground. Looking back, I am certain my Heavenly Father must have directed an angel to pick up that tumbling jeep and set us right. Truly, it was a miracle the jeep did not roll and kill all four of us.

Another divine blessing came into my life soon after that miracle. Scarlet Virginia joined us in the foster home. She was a little older and taller than I was and had blond hair. I learned she had been adopted when she was five years old. After falling into some trouble, she ran away and landed with us. One day as we were talking and getting high downstairs in our room, Rhonda started comparing our stories and the placement of our smallpox-shot scars. As it turned out, Scarlet Virginia was my long forgotten older sister. Her birthday is on February 12, and mine is on February 2, so we are the same age every year for ten days. I thought that was pretty cool.

Naturally, I took her to see our biological mom, but things went sour between Scarlet Virginia and our mother. Soon Scarlet Virginia did not want anything to do with her. Overall, my early teen years were tough. Not only did I find myself in multiple foster homes, but I also spent time in the detention center, basically a jail for youth. I was sent there for shoplifting twice, for being at my natural mom's when I was supposed to be at a foster home, and for running away. I hated the center; every stay there was a demoralizing experience.

Finally, my caseworker, completely fed up with my wild ways, said it was time to place me in better care. I told her if she had another Mormon foster home in mind, I was going to run. I flatly refused to have anything to do with that "church" by that time. To me, it was a place of empty tradition and hypocritical people who knew little of the God they claimed to serve.

When she showed me a one-way ticket to Las Vegas, Nevada, I smiled. I was headed to the Home of Good Shepherds, a Catholic school for girls.

3

The Lord Is My Shepherd

God demonstrates His own love toward us, in that
while we were still sinners, Christ died for us.

—Romans 5:8

I ARRIVED AT the Home of Good Shepherds with the
understanding that I was to get my ninth-grade credits and
stay for a full year.

My first impression of the place was that it looked like a
prison. Surrounded by a fence, it was located in the middle
of the desert. Clearly, it would not be easy to escape from
such a place. On campus sat a Catholic chapel that opened
into off-limits quarters for the nuns, a school, a swimming
pool, and a set of student dormitories watched over by
German Shepherd dogs.

The dorms were formed by cubicles with curtains for
doors. Each student had a bed, a closet, a window, and a
desk. The common areas included a phone-call room, a

living area with a television, a kitchen, and a dining room. I had two beautiful, healthy plants in my room. I was so proud of them. The laundry facility was in another building, and I hated going over there at night because the building was surrounded by bats out on a feed.

The school was an all-girls home, and we each had to contribute to its success by doing chores. Weeding a cactus garden, picking up dog mess, cleaning the chapel, and cooking were some of my responsibilities. On weekdays, we attended classes. At night, we had to sit at the table writing lines and do homework or read. I did well in one class in particular. It taught life skills, such as how to make out checks and find success. Looking back, I'm certain the woman who taught it was a Christian. Her lessons were packed with biblical values, and hers became my favorite class of all.

The school received money from the state; sometimes we could buy extra things or earn phone calls. Off-campus recreation was rarely an option. We would sometimes gather all the dorm girls to watch a movie, but that was about it. Occasionally, however, I was able to earn a trip into town. But I had to go with one of the sisters, and they drove pretty crazily!

Finally, summer break arrived, and I flew back to stay with my half sister Scarlet Virginia in her adopted family's home. I had left my cat, Patches, there and couldn't wait to see him, but was *not* happy to find out he had run away.

Scarlet Virginia introduced me to straight-leg jeans. While I had sworn I would never quit my bell-bottoms, I liked how the straight-legs fit so much I gave up the bell-bottom look forever. Over the coming weeks, we went to a few parties, drank, and did some drugs together. I also met a cousin of her adopted family. His name was Ben, and I quickly decided he was nice looking. By the time I had to fly back to the home, I had developed quite a crush on Ben. I'd even asked if Mr. and Mrs. Roberts, his biological parents, could become my foster parents so I could live with them when I got out of the Home of Good Shepherds.

About the time I got resettled into the home and its routine, my housemom, Miss Kay, asked if I wanted to go to church with her. I liked Miss Kay, who was not one of the nuns. She had taken me to the opera and to a *Nutcracker* ballet. I agreed to go to her church.

We went to an Assemblies of God church as big as a stadium. When worship songs were played, the people around us were raising their hands in praise. I had never seen that before, and it—along with the huge crowd—left me feeling uncomfortable. The service closed with an altar call for anyone who wanted go up to the front to pray and receive Christ. I told Miss Kay there was no way I was going up there. The place was filled with far too many people, and I did not really understand what "salvation" was all about.

Miss Kay meant well, but she often did things I just couldn't grasp. For instance, when something bad happened, she would tell me not to get all worked up about it but just to say, "Praise the Lord!" I'm not sure she understood that because I didn't know Christ, I felt I had no reason to praise Him. Instead, I had long followed my deceptive heart and a lot of worthless traditions passed down to me by my equally lost parents and caretakers.

I had not accepted the Son, so the Spirit was not working in me, helping me walk after the desires of the Father and direct my heart and steps according to His Word. I had no concept of the abundant life she hoped I'd find. I was empty, blind, and deceived. I followed my heart, emotions, and feelings, believing the lies about myself that I'd been told. Many people had put me down. I needed someone to rescue me from the pain, wrong thinking, and poor judgment calls that marked my life. I needed the intervention of my Heavenly Father—not a bunch of platitudes.

To Miss Kay's credit, she continued to pray for me and took me to a smaller church the next week. It had only a few members, and I went to a little class where they explained the salvation invitation. I better understood the Gospel message after sitting in that circle where I was free to ask lots of questions. When the worship service began, I was ready to go up, to "say the prayer," and to give my life over to the Father. To be clear, I still did not know what living like Christ meant, but I was ready to reach out to God for help, if not life direction.

One night soon after that, as I was sitting in my room at my desk, a song came to me. I wrote it down on a piece of paper that I would keep for many years.

When it seems cold and lonely
I found a friend, I found a friend knocking at my door.
I let Him in, and he let out a roar.
He said, "Take my hand, and I will guide you to my
promised land.
Now don't you cry, don't get mad 'cause you will be
glad when I save you in the end.
Whenever you're down, or you need help just give me
a call: I'll make sure you don't fall.
I'm your friend—even after the world comes to an end.
If you are a friend as I am a friend to you, you'll rise again.
My name is God.
Won't you be, my friend?
I will mend your broken heart, even when you're torn
apart by harsh words.
'I Am'
Your Father in heaven.
And I want my sheep together."

Before that encounter, I had felt so alone, abandoned, abused, and rejected. I thought I was a loser and a failure.

I was hard on myself, a critical and negative person. I had wondered what it might be like to end my life because I thought others would be better off without me. But when I came to know God as a friend by placing my faith in Jesus, I began to grasp that the devil had been lying to me. I recognized that God really did love me. While my parents had failed me and other adults had not adopted me, God had filled in the gap and adopted me into His family. I no longer felt abandoned. After years of struggling, I had hope.

Sadly, however, the Gospel message failed to make deep roots in my fifteen-year-old heart. Like the seed that fell on rocky soil in Christ's parable of the Sower in Matthew 13, my walk with Christ started with an initial sprout but failed to take root because it didn't fall on good ground (see vv 20–21). I had ears to hear and could embrace God's love for me. But I had been exposed to the Mormon religion. I was a young teenager carrying a load of baggage...and I simply lacked training in the faith. Consequently, I soon fell away from the truth.

Looking back, I realize my new faith would have been better set to thrive had I been better discipled. I converted to the Christian concept of finding a personal relationship with God through Christ, but I did not become a true *follower* of Christ. I desperately needed to be loved, protected, and guided. I wanted a tangible relationship with the Father. I wanted to hear, "You are beautiful." "You are loved." "You are destined for great things." "God has given you great talents and gifts—you just need help discovering them." I needed to hear those messages so the dry soil of my heart could be nourished. So I could better understand God's heart for me and increase my commitment to Him. I needed someone to come along beside me and help me learn God's Word, but other than a short stretch in a Christian foundations class, I found little guidance.

Sadly, not long after that, I was involved in a fight with another girl who stole my red shirt from the laundry. She refused to give it back to me, and I didn't respond well. A few of us had to weed the cactus garden as discipline, and I threw a big fit over the situation. In the end, I demanded to go home, leaving Home of Good Shepherds three months before completing my time.

One of the housemothers took me to the airport. She said, "Shamara, remember that getting what you want is not always going to work out the way you think it will."

She was right. I needed to learn how to follow wise counsel instead of impulsively doing things my way.

Still, I soon had my ninth-grade credits. About to turn sixteen, I was ready to begin my sophomore year of high school. Prior to the school year, I lived in a shelter home until the Roberts family could qualify for foster care. (I still had my eye on their son, Ben.) Schelley, my caseworker, mentioned putting me in Artec, a boarding home for troubled girls, but I begged her to allow me to go live with the Roberts and go to Outwest High. I also asked for the chance to get good grades.

That last request bought me a trip to see a counselor, who put me on Ritalin. As it turned out, I was ADHD and OCD, and I benefitted from the prescription. For two semesters, I earned a 3.7 average. I was so proud to get five A's and one B! It was the best report card I had ever received. But then I went off Ritalin, and things went downhill. I hung out with potheads, got into another fight, began taking speed, and was nearly raped.

The only high point during this sad time was the summer job I got at the Board of Education. I worked in the textbook area, boxing books, putting them in alphabetical order, and labeling and organizing things throughout the office. I loved it! I was able to buy new clothes, my first ten-speed bike, and an eight-track stereo.

The book of Isaiah says this about Jesus: "For unto us a Son is given…And His name will be called Wonderful, Counselor…" (9:6). How I wish I'd had people in my life to lead me to Jesus as Counselor in those tumultuous teenage years!

I learned early on to dislike traditional therapists. I found them to be more concerned about their time than about me. Those I saw always seemed aloof, cold, unfriendly, detached, reserved, unsociable, cool, and withdrawn. I hated the blank look on their faces as they asked, "How does that make you feel?" I was fully aware of every time their eyes slid to their watches.

I felt so worthless and incompetent in those days and believed I lacked what it took to be truly good at anything. I was a displaced foster child whose caseworker and foster parents had run out of places that would take me. While the counselors tried to help me, they lacked love, compassion, and interest. They never took the time to help me find meaning and purpose. Instead, they'd listen to me for an hour and say, "See you next week."

What I really needed was godly counsel. I needed someone to really hear what I had to say, to wrap her arms around me in love and compassion, and then to point me to God's Word for the answers I needed. I wanted reassurance that God was not mad at me. I needed to know He heard all my thoughts, knew me completely, and loved me anyway. Jesus died because He thought I was worth the sacrifice, and He had a plan and a purpose for me. I, like every other true child of God, was destined for great things. The Lord had placed talents and gifts in me that would allow me to become all He had planned and laid out for me. I needed to hear...

> He does not lead me year by year. Not even day by day. But step by step my path unfolds. My Lord directs my way. Now walk ye in it.

Unfortunately, instead of getting to know the Father's love for me and growing to trust in His purposes and plans, I received a lot of good-intentioned but worldly advice that left me cold. I failed to see how this kind of advice could help me: "What you need is a vacation." "Those boys at school don't really mean you are a 'big fat barrel.' Boys only tease you when they generally like you." Such advice had no place in my reality.

Furthermore, I found no benefit in exercises that encouraged me to draw my family. Which family? It would take me several pages and hours of time to map all those details! Though I already had a royal Father who had adopted me as His own and loved me better than any parents ever would, I continued to long for adoption. No pay-by-the-hour psychologist could fix that.

4

Tough Times and Trouble Follows

> My son, give attention to my words; Incline your
> ear to my sayings. Do not let them depart from
> your eyes…Keep them in the midst of your heart;
> Ponder the path of your feet, And let all your ways
> be established.
>
> —Proverbs 4:20–21, 26

SOMEONE ONCE TOLD me the word *Bible* stands for basic instructions before leaving earth. I wish I had been able to grasp its importance earlier. Throughout high school, I allowed the world to lead me wherever it wanted. I was trained in the school of "how not to live."

Life is full of bad leaders who are more than willing to take a girl in the opposite direction of the path she should choose. Under the influence of such voices, I got into mischief, partied, lived on the edge, and generally fell prey to the father of lies.

Throughout my sophomore and junior years, I was at the Roberts's foster home. For a time, I did well there, enjoying the good grades I was able to make with the help of my Ritalin and spending time with the family's youngest daughter. She played with me and entertained me with her rendition of the hula. I desperately wanted the Roberts (or the Wills family with whom I'd stayed earlier) to adopt me, but that never happened. Mrs. Roberts (Julie) was a petite blonde in her late thirties or early forties; she was diabetic. Her husband, Irvin, was a large man with graying black hair, glasses, and a beard. He loved stray cats, as well as giving me lectures. To this day, I am grateful the family welcomed me to their home and took care of me.

Mart was the couple's oldest son. He looked smart, wore glasses, and got good grades. He also drove an old classic Chevy that we would sometimes take to school. Mart's younger brother, Ben, was the one I'd long considered a total hottie. He lifted weights down in his room and had a lean and muscular frame to show for it. The third son was James; he was around twelve or thirteen. On the chubby side, he had blond hair and blue eyes. He and Nannette, the fourth child in the family, were close. She was around seven when I went to live with them.

The family also had a few pets. Garfield was their fat orange cat. They also owned Spook, an ugly white poodle. Nannette had a parakeet that would occasionally get loose. Irvin taught the bird to fly into the shower so it could get wet and bathe.

On my sixteenth birthday, Julie's mom, whom we all called Nana, gave me a very special gift. She had an old bedroom set with a matching cedar chest, which she called a hope chest. Nana explained that a young woman should have a special place to store her memories while collecting things for her marriage and future. I was absolutely delighted with her gift. It meant a great deal to me, and I still have it. The gift made me feel special and loved, as if I were a daughter who belonged to their family. I loved to look inside it, gazing at the set of real crystal glasses, a scrapbook, and a blanket it contained.

Overall, the adult members of the Roberts family were a positive influence on me, but Ben—my crush—was not. He got high, and I started down that path again. I was frustrated to discover he was easily annoyed with me because I had thought I had sensed vibes of attraction between us. Looking back, I wonder if he was irritated because I asked everyone at school to call me Shamara Roberts, hoping people would assume the popular Ben Roberts was my brother. (He was on the wrestling team at school, and many girls found him attractive.)

Years before, when I had escaped Bernice's abuse for a shelter home, I received a white stuffed dog with red ears. I had named him Spike. Ben noticed him and the other stuffed animals among my things and taught me how to hide my bag of weed inside a toy. Not long after that, his parents found the stash inside Spike, and I was busted.

They told me drugs could never come into the house again. I kept my mouth shut about the drugs I knew were hidden in Ben's room.

That same year, my junior year, I was a reporter for the school newspaper and took a typing class and a class on preparing income tax returns from a teacher I'll call Mr. Clever. He was serious about his job. Sadly, I would often enter his class with a cheat sheet in hand while buzzing on a little high. (It wasn't all that difficult to get high at school, but one time I did have to swallow a joint "roach" because I was about to be busted. From that day on, my name was Roach instead of Shamara.) Anyway, one day, Mr. Clever caught on to my ways and made me retest. Meanwhile, I also tried to cheat in history, but I still got an F. (Yes, I know it is bad when a girl tries to cheat and still gets the answers wrong.) School became increasingly difficult.

I mentioned that I did a lot of partying in this season of my life. Little did I know I was setting myself up for big trouble. One night, I went to a party with my friend Misty. She was meeting a guy there on a blind date, and she wanted me to go along. But once the two met, they soon decided to hook up. They disappeared, leaving me to pass the evening without them.

Right away, I felt uncomfortable in that house. There was an Ouija board on the counter and *Book of Mormon* on the coffee table. Both objects gave me bad vibes. A guy at the party brought me a little green pill (a form of speed, so

I thought. I believe it was a date rape pill.) and suggested I chase it with some whiskey. I followed his instructions, and it wasn't long until I didn't feel so well. I asked if I could go somewhere to pass out. A male voice answered that I could go lie down in the family camper until Misty and her date emerged from the basement.

A little later, I woke up inside the camper to find that the guy who had given me the whiskey and pill was trying to rape me! In my drugged, sleepy voice, I told him to "quit" and "get off me," but he didn't care. What a relief it was when Misty and her guy appeared just in time to stop him and take me home!

I wish I could say my night improved when I got back to the Roberts's house. Instead, I found my foster dad, Irvin, passed out on the front room floor. Apparently, he'd overdone it with alcohol. When I paused to see what was wrong, Ben told me to just stay quiet and go to bed. That dismissal did not set too well with me. I'd been through a lot and needed to talk about it. I told him what had happened and even gave him the first name of my attacker.

"Oh well," he said with a shrug, "that's what you get."

Any feelings I had for Ben shriveled that night. I was so hurt to know he honestly did not care to stand up for me. I could expect no protection—or sympathy—from him.

A few weeks later, I injured my ankle when I slipped on the wet grass as I was running out to the car to get to school. I think my foot twisted and came out of my clog.

Anyway, though I was in a lot of pain, I made it through the day and then went to the doctor. After I'd sat through two x-rays, Dr. Smootch announced that I had broken my anklebone and had torn the tendons in my foot. I had to wear a cast for a while, and the gym teacher was upset that I couldn't participate in class. That, coupled with my terrible grades, was enough to make Julie and Irvin go to bat for me with the school board. After several long, heated discussions, they made a deal that would allow me to write six reports to get my grades up.

Around this same time, I was in a head-on collision with another ten-speed cyclist. I was not the best bike rider in town, and it was hard for me to peddle because I am only a little over five feet tall. Add to that the fact that I hated to keep my pants hemmed up, and I was a rolling recipe for disaster.

The accident happened when an older guy crossed in front of me. Somehow we collided, and I smacked my nose hard on the pavement and tore up my bike. The guy was spitting angry over the wreck and told me to stay on my own street; he clearly did not care that I was hurt. I picked myself up and made the ride home, frowning over my bent handlebars and other damages. It didn't help when my foster brothers laughed at me about the wreck.

I don't know if it was the sting of Ben's rejection, the fact that I had clouded my judgment with drug use, or the naked truth that I just wanted to be loved, but I agreed to become Joel Wick's girlfriend about this time. Joel was the dorkiest person in the tenth grade. I do not know what I saw in him, but he was likeable. Prior to our relationship, I'd been proud to be a virgin. I wanted to stay that way, but some of the other girls at school teased me about it. With their taunts ringing in my ears, I gave myself to Jay.

A little later, he gave me a ring. My foster parents got terribly upset over seeing that little piece of jewelry on my hand, and they told me to take it off and give it back to him. I was not to go steady with him or with anyone else at my young age. I didn't talk back to the Roberts. I knew that would just bring on an immediate reprimand. Instead, I sadly broke it off with Jay and wished I had never listened to those mean girls at school.

A month or two passed and my sister Scarlet Virginia married. She was sixteen at the time, and her husband was a Hispanic man with earrings in both ears. The wedding was held at Granny's house. Granny was Irvin Roberts's mother. She could cook the best strawberry and rhubarb cobbler, and her chicken liver wraps with bacon were addictive! I loved that plump, jolly woman; she was fun. Granny had been to Hawaii twelve times, and I always enjoyed her company.

Looking back, I'd say I thrived best during times of family togetherness. I can't help but wonder whether my teen years might have been less rocky had the Roberts family known the Lord. I really think that ongoing godly guidance and involvement in a good, solid youth group would have gone a long way in keeping me out of trouble.

Unfortunately, trouble was only beginning to mark my young life.

5

Independent Living

If we are faithless, He remains faithful;
He cannot deny Himself.

—2 Timothy 2:13

By the end of my junior year, I had decided I wanted to live on my own. I was seventeen years old. Julie and Irvin tried to talk me out of it, encouraging me to remember I had only a couple of semesters left before graduation. I had promised them I would register for my senior year, and they did their best to see that I did. But I was stubborn and wanted to leave; in the end, I got my way. Irvin warned I couldn't come back to them if I blew it. (They knew I would.)

I foolishly moved in with Vanessa, the sister who had brought me so much trouble since the day we met. During the first weeks of my stay with her, she tried to talk me into joining the army. I failed the tests required for entry and had only stayed with her for about a month when she bailed out on me in the middle of the night. Not only did she leave me the added responsibility of paying her rent, but she also carried some of my things away with her when she moved to another state.

I called my social worker and asked if she could send me a roommate to help pay rent. She responded by sending over a not-terribly-bright teenager named Delanna. When the blonde showed up at my door with a black kitten under her arm, I wondered if it was some sort of omen. While I no longer believed in such things, I was right that the girl would only add new messes to the ones I already faced. She generally lived up to my low first impressions of her.

Summer wound to a close, and it was time to register for my senior year at Grain High School. I showed up for registration, but when I saw the long line and the apparently snooty students who would attend there, I said, "No way," and left.

For a couple of weeks, I continued to work at the Temple State Board of Education. I was still working in the textbook area, and I liked it. My boss's name was Shawanda. She wanted to hire me on full-time as soon as I was eighteen and had graduated. Unfortunately, I called in "sick" a few too many times. One morning, I called in and she warned that I better not miss again. The next day I called, and true to her word, she told me either to come in or to expect to find a pink slip waiting for me the next time

I did. I shamefully said, "I quit." Somehow I felt that was better than getting fired.

Not long after that, I received a lengthy typed letter from Shawanda. In it, she predicted I would turn out like my natural mother: on welfare, having children with different fathers, and generally ending up just like her. The words settled deep in my spirit, and to this day, I wish my old boss had kept her thoughts to herself. But how could she have known how desperately I needed to hear that there was hope for me? She would have helped me far more by sending me a letter of encouragement instead of her ranting. Perhaps something like this: "Shamara, you can succeed. You will undoubtedly suffer consequences because of your decision to leave your job, but I believe you can get back on track" (see James 3:1–10). How sad to predict curses over a teen's life. I so needed hope!

Things weren't going much better for me at my apartment. I got in trouble for having my cats, Budweiser and Michelob, there. The neighbors also complained that we were too loud. I was told to get rid of my pets, so I just let them loose outside and hoped they would be okay. For a while, they came around often, and I fed them. It really grieved me to let them go. I've long been an animal-loving person to mostly cats, birds and horses.

In the coming weeks, I partied a lot, often listening to depressing love songs. One day when I was listening to Van Halen's song "Runnin' with the Devil," I decided I was indeed running with the devil. I was more or less on the highway to hell, and I became increasingly convinced that was where I belonged. I began to sink into depression until I no longer believed my Heavenly Father could love me. Surely He wouldn't want a loser and a reject like me in His family!

Although I now know God was still there in the midst of my chaos, I could no longer feel Him and assumed He had left me. It probably didn't help that I was often high on drugs during that time. I was taking them to kill the pain, but their effects would quickly wear off and I'd feel all that hurt filling me up again. I was depressed and so full of condemnation. I was alone once again with no one to turn to and guide me.

I quickly realized I couldn't pay my bills without the steady income of a job, so Delanna and I spent a whole day searching for work. When we came up empty, we decided to apply for food stamps. As it turned out, we didn't qualify for them because we weren't enrolled in school.

"I'm starving," she admitted. "Let's just go to Sambo's." (Sambo's was a restaurant like Denny's or Village Inn.) "We'll order our food, eat, and make a run for it."

I didn't like the idea. I'd never done anything like that. Still, we went into the restaurant and ate. Then I ordered a dessert. While I was waiting for it, Delanna suggested we should just go ahead and leave. When I hesitated, she scurried out the door. I didn't know what else to do, so I jetted as well.

Soon the police were chasing us, and I felt as if I were running in slow motion. It was the weirdest experience. The officers caught us and recognized me right away from previous encounters when I'd broken curfew. And so, once again, I found myself in detention. Our caseworkers made us sit it out in there for three days.

By this point, I'd had enough of being on my own. I asked my caseworker if she could get me back into the Wills's family house. She made it happen, and I went back to that family for the third time. I started attending school and things began to improve, though there was still plenty of drama along the way.

Sometimes I look back on the decisions I've made in life and wonder how I could have ever made some of the choices. Not long after I'd moved in with the Willses, I made one of my poorest.

As I've stated, my biological mother had issues and was not of sound mind. Her parenting skills were twisted, though I don't think she intended me harm when she decided I needed a new man in my life. She took me to a family funeral—of all places—with the goal of hooking me up with her latest husband's nephew, an unhappily married man.

As mourners gathered to feast and drink, I was introduced to Oscar. He was twenty-three, and at first I shrugged off his advances by telling him I didn't go out with married guys. He continued to call me over the coming weeks, however, insisting he would be divorced in three months and then we could be together.

I had my cap and gown ordered for graduation from Jordon River High. It was December of 1981, and Christmas break had just begun. I remember thinking how much I wanted to graduate and hold that diploma in my hand. I'd been trying extra hard to fit in at school and had begun to weave new dreams for my future. I wanted to become a counselor or social worker so I could be understanding, compassionate, and empathetic to others who walked paths similar to mine.

I was crushed the day my foster mom delivered the truth I'd refused to see. I was failing. I didn't have the grades to graduate that year. While she would later apologize, she also kicked me out of that foster home. I went to a shelter home instead and began telling myself that I was in love. I wrote a sugar letter to Oscar, and in it, I must have said "I love you" in every other sentence. Without anyone to give me wise advice, I started to think a life with him was my only hope for a happy future.

Assuming that my foster parents were done with me for good, I decided to push myself a little more aggressively on Oscar. He was surprised the day I showed up at his doorstep. To make a long story short, I ended up living at his parents' house until I was about four months pregnant with Oscar's child. I was willing to overlook the facts that at the age of eighteen, I was living with a family of alcoholics and pinning my hopes on a married man of twenty-four. I had no job. I'd given up my schooling and career goals. I wasn't even entirely sure if Oscar would choose his wife or me in the long run.

One day, Oscar's spouse and I got together and cornered him. We told him it was time to make up his mind. He played us both, still refusing to make the call; she spent part of the meeting calling me a list of names—ugly but fitting and deserved.

After that, my stepmother, Patty, who spent a lot of time in the local bar, told me about her friend Brian, who had a split-level house. I could pay rent and stay there. That sounded like a good idea, so I moved again. Oscar would come to visit and drink Brian's booze.

When I was about eight months along, Oscar decided he'd had enough of our relationship. He said, "You're too good for me." The truth was that he'd started seeing another young girl.

I'd fallen for a man with the full knowledge that he was cheating on his wife. I should have known he would cheat on me just as easily. Still, I was hurt by his actions. During the course of our relationship, I had expected him to love me faithfully and to give our child stability. What I didn't know then was that a man does not change because a woman loves him, is intimate with him, or has his baby. A man changes because he wants to change—and Oscar did not.

If I had known to find my worth not in what other people said to me or in how they treated me but in what God's Word says about me, I could have welcomed my baby girl into a much brighter world.

6

Broken Heart
and Dreams Torn Apart

Keep your heart with all diligence,
for out of it spring the issues of life.

—Proverbs 4:23

I LOVED RANI Anna Faith from the moment I knew she
was developing inside me. How I enjoyed feeling her
heartbeat, her hiccups, and the huge flip she made when
she went into position for delivery! My doctor expected
her to arrive on October 12, 1982, but I didn't go into labor
until six days later.

Oscar found out I was in the hospital, and he left his
new girlfriend's side long enough to come by and irritate
me. "Hurry up and push that baby out," he ordered, without
an ounce of sympathy or compassion. I wanted to smack
him as I lay there in a sweat and he jawed on and on about

his "rich chubby girl" and "her daddy's truck." I'm not sure he realized I was in labor with *our* daughter.

What a rush it was to hold Rani in my arms for the first time. Within a day of her arrival, I could identify her cry among the others from down the hall. Her little wail, "la—la—la," was musical. I should have known right way that she was purposed to sing.

When we were released from the hospital, Mom took me to her house. While that may not sound like a wise move on my part, I needed someone to show me how to bathe Rani, to lay her down on a different side each time, and how to swaddle her in a blanket. My ignorance about things like that made me lean on my mom for support.

I remember the day when Rani and I went to my own place. I loved holding her! It was so wonderful to have just the two of us there together. Frankly, I still remember those days as being some of the best moments of my life.

One afternoon when Rani was under a month old, I was feeding her. She gagged, and the sound terrified me. She seemed to be having difficulty breathing. I told Mom—I was talking with her on the phone when it happened—and she called an ambulance. A paramedic came and cleared the baby's passageway. Then they carried her into the back of the ambulance, and I scrambled into the front seat. By this time, she had stopped breathing.

We got to the hospital, and I prayed like I had never prayed. I begged God not to let me lose her. Little did I know this wouldn't be the first time Satan tries to destroy my daughter. A mother's prayers are vital. She was so precious and small! The doctors ran tests and discovered she had reflux. They gave me a slanted board to position her on as she slept, and then they sent us home.

Not long after that, my oldest sister, Vanessa, came over and said she needed a place to stay. She was about three months pregnant, and I let sympathy override the fact that her history was one of surrounding me in trouble, lies, deception, and manipulation. How naive I was to let her in the door at all! Regardless, I allowed her to live in Brian's home with me. A month later, she had managed to run Brian's phone bill up to three hundred dollars. I was so angry; I didn't know how I was going to pay Brian for that bill.

On another occasion, Vanessa and I were hanging out with Brian's son, Louie, who had just moved into another vacant room in the house. Somehow the three of us decided that doing damage to Oscar's girlfriend's truck would be a great idea. We went to the place where she worked and put a potato in the exhaust pipe and sugar in the gas tank. Almost immediately, I felt terrible. I'd never vandalized anyone's property. Worse, we soon discovered it was her dad's vehicle and not hers.

Vanessa tried to pin the blame on Louie and me, attempting to make it look as if she'd had no part in the matter. In the end, though, all three of us received fines and some jail time. Oscar had to watch Rani for the two days I was in jail. Thankfully, the judge suspended eight of the ten days of our sentences because Vanessa and I were mothers.

That one weekend in jail was enough to convince me I never wanted to return there. I was scared and demoralized when I had to take off my clothes in front of the guards and allow them to spray me down with insecticide. I hated that I had to wear the ugly jail clothes too. Add to this the fact that a mean lesbian woman and another threatening inmate scared me as I ate my meals. I quickly discovered that hard-timers do not like small-timers—especially when they are booked for something trivial.

Understandably, Brian insisted that we move out of his place after the incident, and I had to find a suitable new apartment in a hurry. I found a place I could afford on welfare assistance, but it was a far cry from nice. It was a one-bedroom studio apartment without doors; the bathroom was the size of a closet. Apparently, the space had once been a trolley car, and it didn't look very homey. I fixed it up as best I could and borrowed a broom to sweep the carpet every now and then.

Rani was in cloth diapers during this time, and I had to wash them by hand. I'd boil wash water on the gas stove as she lay in her port-a-crib, which the Roberts family had given to me. It was a lot of work to care for both of us in that rough little place, but every day I spent with my precious daughter, I learned determination and perseverance. My baby girl was such a gift.

By the time Rani was about three months old, I'd begun obsessing over the fact that Oscar wouldn't take me back and give our beautiful little girl his love and name. I wanted to share moments with him and wondered why he didn't care about us. Why would he not make us his family?

I only wish I'd been reading my bible in those days. God's Word is so clear that He is "a father [to] the fatherless… God sets the solitary in families" (Ps. 68:5–6). Yet instead of finding that message and taking it to heart, I set out to fix my problems on my own.

In those days, I was a big fan of amphetamines because I enjoyed being thin and having energy; I had struggled for a long time with a weight complex, so the pills seemed like a solution. I met a man, Brett, who looked like a shorter version of Sylvester Stallone. He was about six years older than I was and was covered in tattoos, but he had one thing going for him: he could provide me with speed.

One evening, he asked if I would lie on the floor next to him. I didn't own a bed. I had one couch, and Vanessa's sister, Susanna, was sleeping on it. I did what he asked, and the guy soon became like a stray that wouldn't leave. Not only would he eat my food, but he would also pull the suicide card on me: "I will kill myself if you don't let me stay. I will stab myself right here." I told him to do it outside then because I didn't want his blood all over my place. I was growing impatient with him, hoping he would move on soon. My patience wore out, however, when he began flicking my sweet baby girl in her tender temple.

Desperate, I made a phone call I would regret for the rest of my life. I called Rani's Aunt Mara, who was Oscar's aunt, and asked her for advice. I explained that Brett's actions toward Rani were harmful and cruel. I needed someone to keep her for a couple of days so I could kick him out.

What I didn't realize when I picked up the phone was that Aunt Mara had been waiting for just such an opportunity.

I washed Rani's clothes and made sure she had enough diapers and formula to make it for a week without me. I took her over to her grandparents' home and gave them instructions on her feeding times, explaining that she had a doctor's appointment that following Wednesday. I planned to take her home afterward.

Oscar took me back to my place and warned I wouldn't get Rani back until Brett was gone. I replied, "No problem." I completely agreed.

I went to the doctor's office on Wednesday to see Rani through her appointment and then take her home. I knew something was wrong when Oscar, his brother Tyler, and his girlfriend all came to join us. They waited for me to finish up at the doctor's office—probably to make sure I was not going to run off with her. After that, Oscar wrenched her from my arms and left me standing in the parking lot, screaming, devastated, and without an ally. Rani was gone, and I desperately wanted her back.

I told the police what happened, and they asked me whether Oscar's name was on the birth certificate. It was, and that made our situation a civil matter instead of a criminal one. *Great.* I sighed at the news. *Like I can afford an attorney.*

I cannot explain the pain I went through in the days that followed. It was torture not to be able to take care of my daughter. I wondered whether Oscar's family would care for her as I would, but I suspected they would not. Aunt Mara's house was dirty, and I just knew she wouldn't clean up the place for the sake of my small baby.

I cried so hard and tried pleading with them. I was willing to do anything I could to get her back. Once I even considered trying to kidnap her and make a run for it, but Rani was heavily guarded by her cousins and aunt. I ached inside but was powerless to gain control of the situation. What a nightmare to be separated from my greatest joy! And if all that weren't bad enough, I lost the financial assistance that came with mothering her. I lost my baby and within a month, my home.

The situation worsened when I found out my one night of sleeping with Brett had led to the coming of another baby. Brett, who didn't have a job, wanted me to hitchhike to Wyoming with him to meet his dad. I agreed to go there temporarily since I was homeless, but I was painfully aware

I had to be back for court soon to gain temporary custody of Rani. I expected a brief trip.

Brett had failed to tell me the state of Wyoming closes its roads in bad winter weather. I was horrified to find myself miles away from my baby as our court date approached and then passed. I was nineteen and hurting; no one understood my pain, and no one cared how I felt. I wanted my little girl. I just knew she needed her mom, and I knew what was best for her. No matter where we went during that awful period, I would see moms holding their baby girls and I would sob. The pain and guilt nearly consumed me.

Brett didn't care about my worries, but he did keep me distracted. He gave me a tattoo, and he insisted that I climb White Mountain with him. (Of course, it was covered in snow and ice, and I broke my tailbone in the process.) Though his dad helped get me out of Wyoming as soon as possible, we were too late to change what happened. I'd been gone for three months.

I scrambled to my hearing and discovered that just as Aunt Mara's lawyer had suggested to them, the court felt I'd abandoned my child. Looking back, I suppose I had not managed to look responsible enough to meet my daughter's needs; therefore, my attorney wasn't too eager to stand up for me. I wasn't treated like an adult that day; everyone spoke to me as an irresponsible nineteen-year-old accused of neglecting my infant. I was denied rights to Rani. Just like that, I lost my baby. Rani's Aunt Mara even denied me the right to see her much of the time. Thankfully, Oscar stepped in to allow me occasional visits.

Oscar let me visit Rani at his parents' house a few times, though they never made it easy for me to spend time with her. I desperately wanted to get back with him to somehow make things right. It seemed that if I could just paste our little family together, everything would be all right, so I tried telling Oscar that the baby I carried was his. Of course, he didn't believe me. I wondered how I could take another step without having our little girl home in my arms. Apparently, I couldn't now that someone else's child was very obviously on the way.

When I was eight months pregnant, I was staying with my mom. Oscar, who did not want to deal with the hassle of weaning Rani off the bottle, had dropped her off with me. Delighted, I called my attorney, through Legal Aide, who said to keep her in my care until the day of the hearing. (Oscar's custody over her was not yet complete.) I kissed her sweet cheeks and smiled. "Finally," I said, "a chance to get you back!"

Mom and I headed to the store to pick up some baby food and a few other things I thought we might need. Rani was sitting in the shopping cart, crying to be picked up. I reached for her sweet little arms, ready to embrace her and reassure her that everything was okay. My mother, however, became hostile and demanded that I put her in the cart and let her scream. "You cannot hold her," she barked at me in a tone that left no room for argument. "You are pregnant, and you might wrap the cord around your baby's neck." She jerked the cart from me, and I retreated to the baby food aisle.

Moments later, I returned to see my mother hitting my eleven-month-old, not with her hand but with her fist! I was horrified, rushing to intervene and so upset that I thought I would be sick there in the aisle. Worse still, a store employee had already reported that she'd seen Mom brutally punch my daughter in the head and had called the police. We were escorted to the back of the store, and Mom was arrested.

The police officer asked where I lived. When I replied that I lived with my mother, he informed me that he would have to remove my daughter from my care. It simply wasn't safe to keep a baby around my mom. He looked at me as if I should have known that.

I felt the room spin at this news. How could she do such a thing to me? Mom knew this had been my only chance to get my daughter back, and she had ruined it! While a part of me wanted to press charges and let her do a year in jail for what she did to my baby, I knew that wouldn't solve anything. Instead, they let her off with a fine and a permanent child abuse record. After that incident, Rani was gone—and I couldn't do anything about it.

Though I returned to court several times trying to get custody of my daughter, I lost every time. I missed the chance to do her hair, to watch her grow, and to put her in dance and gymnastics classes. Worse, I lost the opportunity to hold her and tell her how much I love her. I didn't get the chance to wipe her tears, to care for her when she was sick, or to say prayers with her at night. I would not really get to know my child until she was almost an adult.

Deeply discouraged by losing Rani, I tried to focus on my coming baby. Brett told me about a Christian shelter for boys that may put us up because we had no money and no place to live. They agreed to the plan on one condition: we had to get married before we could live together under their roof.

In fairness, the shelter had no idea about the then-completely-platonic nature of our relationship. They assumed we were a boyfriend and girlfriend who had conceived our baby in love and affection for each other. They couldn't know that the thought of marrying my baby's father made me sick to my stomach.

I knew he'd made babies with plenty of other women, and his irresponsible habits and emotional outbursts repeatedly played in my mind like scenes from a bad movie. What an awful sentence to have to marry someone I so disliked! I could barely tolerate him and the ugliness of his body covered in tattoos. (I am not judging you if you have tattoos; I personally do not find them appealing.)

Still, because it was so cold and I would deliver in about four months, I figured I had to comply. I felt as if I had run out of options.

Some might wonder why I didn't just abort the baby to rid myself of the whole mess. First, even at my lowest, I felt that every child was a gift from the Heavenly Father. No child is to blame for his or her parents' actions. Second, I honestly loved each baby the Lord developed in my womb. They were just as much a part of me as were my own limbs. How could I possibly destroy them? (Abortion is an inhumane act of murdering an infant. God does not make mistakes, and He makes it clear in His written word that murder is wrong. "Thou shall not kill.")

I found it terrifying to think of giving them up at all. I'm reminded of the time a social worker asked me to give up Brett's child for adoption. When I told her no, she asked me what I could possibly offer the child. I replied from my heart, "I have love, and I will do the best I can for this baby."

Just as our new landlords had requested, I reluctantly married Brett. When our wedding pictures were developed, I smirked to discover our heads had been cut off in every shot. (It seemed appropriate.) Brett and I lived together as newlyweds for about a month before he received a phone call from my eldest sister, Vanessa. She wanted him to go see her newly arrived baby, Brianna—the child she had been carrying during her disastrous stay with me.

I went with him and was surprised to discover that this latest addition was half sister to the baby swelling *my* middle. As it turned out, Vanessa was actually married to Brett! That meant my "husband" had committed not just adultery with me but also bigamy. When I went to an attorney to get an annulment, I was told I hadn't been legally married after all. Brett hadn't bothered to have the ceremony put on record. That figured since bigamy is illegal.

I was so happy to be free ofBrett that I didn't much care about his lies. Our entire "marriage" had been a joke. I wanted a marriage of commitment and love. What a relief to learn I'd never been truly married in the first place! For a while, I tried living in one studio apartment and then another before I eventually settled at a place on the west side of town, right next to the overpass. The house fit my budget and had a spacious living area and a place for my bed and the coming baby's crib. It had a good-sized kitchen with an old-fashioned tub in the bathroom. The main thing I did not like about it, however, was that it was cold, and I was afraid to light its old gas furnaces. I didn't care for all the cockroaches running around the place either.

It gets so cold in Mormonville. Some days I felt as though the winter wind and snow would turn me into an ice pop or a snow woman if I stood still too long. I tried to fill my belly with affordable foods like liver and onions and ramen noodles with veggies before making my daily trips to ride the city transit system. It was seldom punctual or dependable, and most of the time, I could have walked to my destination before the bus arrived, but it was the only transportation I had. Each time I headed to the station, my feet got wet and then started to freeze as I cupped my hands and blew warm breath into them, trying to keep my mind off the cold. I remember how exhausted I'd be by the time the bus arrived. It was so disheartening that few people on the crowded bus bothered to give up their seats so my pregnant belly and swollen ankles could have a rest.

I was on my own, and I needed assistance. Though I am not a fan of the LDS occult of religion for many reasons, I do credit them with assisting me during those difficult months. They asked me to volunteer at the store warehouse and to go to a Mormon church. In return, they helped meet my basic needs as I waited for my baby's arrival. They paid my gas and rent in those first difficult months.

Sadly, however, I found that most Mormon churchgoers were judgmental, critical, and even cruel at times. I was often asked, "What do you do?" I was on welfare. "Where do you live?" I lived in a bad part of town. "What do you drive?" I didn't. "Where is the father of your baby?" He was married to my sister. "What religion are you?" Though not practicing, I considered myself more Christian than Mormon. "Did you graduate?" No. "Why does your daughter not live with you?" That answer was best kept to myself.

It didn't take long for me to realize I was an outcast among their group. Seemingly religious people neither supported me emotionally nor accepted me for who I was; instead, they told me I had to dress a certain way, that I couldn't wear a cross around my neck, and that I had to sing certain hymns. Then they generally made me feel as if I could never reach the Father—no matter how hard I may try. (Religions make you conform; following Jesus transforms you to be more like Him.)

"God," I prayed through my tears, "help me! Please, won't You help me?"

7

A Hopeless Situation?

My son, if sinners entice you, do not consent.

—Proverbs 1:10

In Jeremiah 29:11, the Lord declares to His people, "For I know the thoughts that I think toward you…thoughts of peace and not of evil, to give you a future and a hope."

As I shivered in my little home by the overpass and struggled to find good in the midst of all I faced, I did not know God had never stopped loving me—no matter how I had failed. In fact, He was willing not only to forgive me for my recent mess-ups but also to help me find my way despite them. To give me a hope and a future.

No matter how hopeless my situation seemed, no matter how undeserving of His love I felt, I was no different from the son in the parable of the Prodigal Son. And God—just like the father in that story—was waiting to welcome me home.

My sins, however, weighed heavily on me in those cold days of November. I felt alone. Forgotten. Nothing in my life was going according to plan.

My midwives predicted that Brutus's baby would be born on November 27, 1983. Right on time, my contractions began. I was with Mom at her Mormon church. We hurried to her house to grab what we needed and called an elderly friend, Old Man Dean, to take us to the hospital in his Pinto.

As we stood on the porch and waited for his customary fight with the stick shift so he could get the car in place to pick us up, Mom told me I should push the next time I felt a contraction. That sounded logical at the time, though it would have been wiser to wait until I reached the hospital. As soon as I bore down against the pain, my water broke. Nothing I did could stop that water: it leaked all over Old Man Dean's car, all across the hospital floor, and it left a huge puddle in the elevator.

Nurses set me up in a room before dilating my cervix with medication and insisting that I wear an oxygen mask. I was supposed to deliver in that room, but the baby started losing oxygen, so they moved me to the delivery room and pulled him out.

Bren had a cone-shaped head and was black and blue. I started crying, horrified that he was either dying or might turn out as physically unattractive as I by then found his dad. Bren also had jaundice, and the poor little guy had to spend hours under an ultraviolet light. But I soon decided he was actually beautiful, and my heart swelled with compassion for my brave little boy who'd faced such a rocky start.

I felt desperate as Bren Ashton and I left the hospital. What would I do? How would I support him on my own? As much as I disliked Brett, I knew he and Vanessa were about to finalize their divorce. I told myself it couldn't hurt Bren Ashton to have his dad around. (Lies from the devil. He is the father of all lies.) Although I was not physically attracted to the guy, I knew he once again needed a place to stay, and our baby needed a father.

A few days later, I sat inBrett's car, discussing our future. Because Bren Ashton continued to need ultraviolet treatments at the hospital, we needed to stick close to the facility. Brutus seemed to think we could just live in his car for a few days. I told him I did not intend to do such a thing, and I was irritated that he would suggest it.

By the time my baby boy was one month old, we were settled back at my place, and he was sleeping through the night. I'd spent the day taking care of him and enjoying one of Rani's rare visits with us.Brett had spent the day with us too; he was always needy and clingy. On that particular afternoon, he'd also demonstrated his selfishness. Rani wanted some of the potato chips he was eating, and that grown man refused to share a couple with her. Brett left the house, and I sighed.

Earlier in the day, Rani had burned her hand pretty badly on the old heater. Long after she was safely home and

Bren was asleep, Oscar arrived. He literally came unglued about the burn, and he took all his anger out on me. (By this time, he was constantly badgering me about having Rani's last name changed from my maiden name to his last name. He was also growing increasingly cruel and insensitive as he gave more of himself over to alcoholism.) Though I was still healing from Bren's birth, Oscar forced himself on me—a situation that would repeat itself over the coming months.

Because of these rapes, I contracted pelvic inflammatory disease (PID), which is an infection of the reproductive organs that can cause sterility. I wound up at Mom's, hoping for help. Instead, I was blackmailed and mistreated. She made my son and me sleep on the kitchen floor, where there was no heat at night. Bren was only four or five months old.

Each day, Mom would vacuum the house, insisting that I stay outside while she did. On her orders, I reluctantly left Bren lying in a little nest I had made for him in the kitchen so he could continue his afternoon naptime. One day when Mom finally let me back in the house, I picked Bren up from the floor. Immediately I noticed he had a large bump on the side of his head; she had smacked him with the vacuum. I felt sick.

Within the week, Bren and I moved in with my new guy friend Taylor. (We'd met at a party where he had found me drunk and then helped me sober up before he took me back to Mom's.)

One night when Taylor was out of town, Oscar came over. I told him I didn't want him, but he had been drinking and wouldn't hear anything I had to say. He raped me again, even as his child by yet another woman grew in her belly.

When Taylor returned, I told him what had happened. He and Oscar got into a fight, and Taylor got Oscar pretty good. Looking back, I realize that Taylor looked out for me and was generally a better guy than the others I had kept company with, but we soon broke up and I moved out. Bren was about seven months old at that time. To this day, I'm not sure why I left Taylor.

Whatever wise decision-making skills I'd had seemed to disappear over the following months of my life. Again and again, I was enticed by people bent on leading me astray, and again and again I gave in to their promises and adopted their ways. After I left Taylor, Bren and I moved in with some neighbors. They were liars and partiers, but I didn't care. Instead, I began looking for direction by having my cards read, which I would later learn is a foolish thing to do (see Deut. 18:10–12; Lev. 19:31). I also continued partying, hooking up with a person named Will. I knew he was a player, but I found him such an intoxicating mix of "cool" and "hot" that I really didn't care.

Shortly after I met Will, Bren and I followed our friend Wanda when she moved into a three-bedroom apartment. Bren was just starting to get around in his walker and to play with the toilet paper. It was tight in that place: we constantly tripped over all our combined belongings and tried to make room for a baby on the move. It didn't help that my baby boy had developed a habit of biting my big toe every time he could get to it!

That August, I had a doctor's appointment. I learned I was eleven weeks pregnant, and I had no doubt the baby was Oscar's. Rani would have a full-blood sibling! Just the thought made me want my firstborn baby girl back so much I could barely stand it. About that time, I decided to take Bren Ashton and Rani to Kansas City, Missouri, where my dad lived. I tried not to think about the fact that I'd have to kidnap Rani to pull off my plan, and I bought tickets and packed as if that were not a factor. Upon my arrival at the airport, however, I was informed that I had only paid for one child, and Bren was too big to be considered a lap baby. Horrified that I had been quoted the wrong price for three tickets, I knew I'd have to leave one of the kids behind with Wanda.

I passed my sweet boy into that woman's care, apologizing that so many of his things were still in our suitcase on the plane. She assured me she'd take care of him, and I trusted her to look after both Bren and our belongings back at the apartment. As Rani and I boarded, I cried at the thought of leaving my baby boy, but I told myself I would be back soon.

Hours later, after our flight, a long stretch of (six hours) sitting in the airport, and another six hours ride in an uncomfortable truck, I made it to Dad's place. Things went poorly from the start. I got eaten up with chigger and fleabites. Dad insulted my baby by calling him Humpty Dumpty. And I miscarried. All I could think was that I wanted to get back to Bren. I missed him so much it hurt.

Within a couple of days after we got to Dad's, Oscar called. He accused me of kidnapping and informed me that Bren Ashton was not with Wanda. She had called family services the very night we'd parted in the airport, telling them I had left him. Only Oscar's intervention kept me from losing him entirely. After that, Wanda had gotten rid of everything the kids and I owned—including my old hope chest!

Oscar hopped a plane and brought Bren to me. I gave him Rani. And despite all the ways that man had hurt me, I found I wanted him back. I didn't love his ways, but I couldn't seem to stop loving him.

For a while, Oscar and I lived together in a fourplex. He took me to the place where my stuff had been sent, and I was at least able to reclaim the hope chest. Life with Oscar, however, was not what I'd hoped. He pawned my ten-speed bike (the one I'd purchased when I was seventeen), and he gave me crabs on multiple occasions.

Once when Oscar was out on a drinking binge, a drunken Indian wandered into our apartment late one night (Oscar had left the door unlocked). I managed to get that strange intruder out, but I was more than a little scared by the incident. I suspected that Brutus, who I knew was into witchcraft and voodoo, had put a spell on me. *Perhaps,* I reasoned, *that's why I am facing such drama.*

When three black widows showed up in our place in one day, I walked to where Brutus was living and told him to leave us alone. Then I hung a wooden "The Lord is my Shepherd" plaque on a wall in our home. Though I wasn't walking with the Lord, I did not doubt His power over evil.

Oscar and I couldn't make our second attempt at a relationship work, and I ended up in a shelter for women and children. Called Marillac, it sat behind a huge cathedral. The place was very strict. Each woman had duties to perform, counseling sessions to attend, and steps she had to take to get back on her feet. Marillac taught me how to properly make up a bed, how to be a better cook, and how to take care of big housecleaning chores like disinfecting walls. I liked what I learned there, and I was so happy to find that Rani was able to stay there with Bren Ashton and me on weekends.

Bren was about twelve months old and Rani was two, though her little body was so petite she was still able to wear twelve-month clothing. Bren Ashton was a chubby, sweet-tempered baby—everyone loved him. The kids thrived under all the attention they received there.

Most days passed uneventfully for us, but one time I had kitchen duty and had to ask someone to keep an eye on the two children. My babies managed to sneak away from their sitter and into a room with a sink. The two caused a flood that soaked the bathroom on the floor underneath them. I had to pay to rent a steam vacuum to suck a good two inches of water out of the carpet!

January 1985 arrived, and it was time to leave Marillac. I had secured a job at the Salty City Egg Plant and had found a tiny apartment Bren Ashton and I could share. It was a finished attic space in a big house across from the Bird Park. It included a fridge, stove, and one bed. The closet was so roomy that I made it Bren's play area.

I rented the space from a man named Mr. O'Neil and felt it was a good buy for the price. An added bonus to living there was that I gained a new friend: Daffy, my landlord's oldest daughter. She became like a daughter to me, and she absolutely loved Bren and watched him many times.

Meanwhile, things had soured between Oscar and me. One time he found me sleeping, apparently overdosed on the antidepressants he knew I took. Rather than trying to wake me, he declared me "stupid" and went on with his day. Another time he got angry at me for not wanting to watch Rani so he could go out with his best friend, Rob. I had my hands full and didn't see the point of taking on additional childcare duties just so he could go out to party and get drunk—again. He responded by pulling back his fist and hitting me on the right side of the face so hard that my jaw broke. It would never be the same.

Each day I took a bus back and forth to the egg plant. Before that, I'd drop Bren off at day care. It was always a tricky thing to pull off because the boss had absolutely no tolerance for late clock-ins.

When I had worked there less than two months, I fell head over heels for a young man with dark hair and eyes. I could not believe it when he liked me too! Our budding relationship definitely made that job worth going to every day. He owned a Honda motorcycle, and we began riding it to work together each morning. Getting Bren to day care became easy: we got him a little leather coat to wear and we just seated him between us.

The job was difficult because it was so tedious. I sometimes fell asleep in the egg-break room where I sat for three hours at a time, watching egg yolks for signs of bloody or black centers. The QA inspector caught me dozing and said if she found me falling asleep again, I'd face the consequences. Butch, whose job it was to routinely hose down the floors in an adjoining room, started squirting me with the hose water to keep me awake.

Six months into the job, I was offered a new position at Bren's day care. They said they'd pay me a salary if I would come help them at their newly remodeled center. Knowing that the deal would put an end to my separation from Bren, I jumped at the chance. Sadly, they soon had to let me go because of financial difficulties within the business.

Benjamin and I had our own place by this time. We rented a cute two-bedroom, and I was able to cook my first turkey there that Thanksgiving. When Benjamin asked me to marry him and gave me beautiful rings, I immediately said yes!

I was brokenhearted when he started trading time with Bren and me for the chance to hang out on State Street. I knew his friends took him down there to get high and chase women. It wasn't long before I demanded that he choose them or us. He moved to another building in the same apartment complex. The engagement ended.

Once again, I faced the predicament of trying to pay rent by myself. I had a new job at Chuckie Ramo restaurant, but I didn't make enough to cover all the rent. I loved working hard there, but I didn't care too much for the dress I had to wear. I did dessert prep in the mornings and then kept the counter stocked and clean and cashiered occasionally.

Anyway, I knew I would need help with my bills, and Vanessa's sister, Susanna, was the only person I could think to ask to move in with me. On the plus side, Susanna—who was my half sister—had a job, but she was also a major partier and only seventeen.

Each day, I walked Bren to his new day care before continuing to work. I had to work weekends and holidays, but I managed. Bren was the highlight of my days. (I would see Rani occasionally when her dad wanted to drop her off, and I always had a bed for her wherever I lived). How I looked forward to heading out the door, picking him up at day care, and then being home with my little man! Bren was rarely ever sick. He looked like Spanky from *The*

Little Rascals, all blond hair and blue eyes. He was smart, humorous, talented, and so adorable that he gave me plenty of smiles. Knowing how dangerous a young man with a great smile can be, I nicknamed him "Trouble." I should have called him clever, tenderhearted, bright, lovable, generous, creative, talented, and artistic. He is all those things and so much more.

When I grew tired of Susanna's constant partying, I moved to a one-bedroom apartment where Bren and I wouldn't need to have a roommate. Unfortunately, I also continued a habit I'd started during my days with Benjamin, taking uppers and downing up to six pink hearts in the morning before chasing them with a Dr. Pepper at work. One day, I even had a bad trip on acid and realized I simply could not be a fit parent if I were to continue with my drug use.

"God," I prayed, in what had become a rare acknowledgment of His existence, "please help me quit." I'm so thankful He answered, and I was able to get over the habit. Had I been willing to seek His guidance about my relationships in that same instance, I believe He would have prevented my next decision.

Susanna, by then on her own, was making regular trips to the prison to see her boyfriend, Lonnie. She came up with the fabulous idea of hooking me up with Shady, who was also doing time. He seemed nice at our first encounter. Together Susanna and I talked Old Man Dean into driving us to the prison on visiting days. I'd either leave Bren in my brother's care or would take him with me.

It wasn't long before I began to smuggle drugs, hidden inside deflated balloons, to Lonnie and Shady. Those two smooth-talkers played us both like fiddles, using us to carry weed and alcohol and provocative pictures in to them and not caring a cent if we got caught in the process. One day, I actually hid their junk inside my son's coat pocket. Shady was busted with the stuff later, and I was questioned. I'm thankful to God I got off with suspended visitation rights because the warden happened to be off duty that day. I never had anything to do with Shady again.

The whole ordeal reminded me I needed to focus on my baby, Bren. As I ran my hand through his beautiful blond hair, I frowned. I didn't want him to be an only child. I wanted another baby. A playmate for my sweet son. Perhaps another child could solve all my troubles.

8

Jeb, Ethan, and God's Provision

Love suffers long and is kind; love does not envy;
love does not parade itself, is not puffed up; does
not behave rudely, does not seek its own, is not
provoked, thinks no evil.

—1 Corinthians 13:4–5

IN 1986, I learned I had severe endometriosis. It seemed my dreams of giving Bren a sibling would never become a reality.

By this time, Bren was about three, and I had an opportunity to go to driving school. Before that, I had never driven, largely because I'd never had a car. How excited I was to learn how to drive before my twenty-first birthday. I still didn't have a vehicle, but I was hopeful that little detail would work itself out over time.

Almost as soon as I entered the driving academy, my eyes were drawn to a gorgeous young man sitting in the back. He was cutting up with a girl I soon learned was his sister. Jared was only eighteen, but I thought he was nice looking, and I wasn't concerned about our age difference. I began talking with him as soon as I got the chance and eventually revealed that I lived by myself with my small son.

Jared seemed completely impressed by my maturity and was drawn to the fact that I *seemed* to have it all together. In no time, we were dating and then sleeping together without fear of pregnancy. (Sadly, it was the very outcome my mother had predicted when I first mentioned Jared— an outcome I'd honestly planned to avoid.)

Soon Jared began staying at my place periodically. He wanted to become a paramedic to better provide for his two little girls from a previous relationship. (He'd fathered his first child at age fourteen.) At first, everything about our relationship seemed great. Then one day, I got a letter from his mother with fifty dollars tucked inside. She thanked me for keeping Jared at my place. *That is odd*, I thought.

Not long after the note arrived, I woke up in the middle of the night and went into the living room to turn off the TV. I was horrified to find Jared on the couch with my youngest sister. (They weren't paying any attention to the television, and this was not her first time to do something like this. She had slept with Oscar and Brett also. Seems Brett had been with three sisters.) I told them to get out and took some pleasure in their scramble to rush out the door, but I knew I had created a whole new level of mess: shockingly, I was pregnant with Jeb's child.

I decided to stay with Jared, hoping he would somehow miraculously change. We found a bigger apartment, and I turned twenty-two. Nevertheless, nothing improved with the passing of time. In fact, I soon realized he was both schizophrenic and incapable of being faithful. It grew clear that Jared had some serious addiction problems. Oscar was an alcoholic and Brett an addict. One day he actually *snorted* pain pills, and I had to call the paramedics to take him to the hospital.

I tried borrowing a car so I could get my drive time in for class, but I ended up hitting a curb and putting a bulge in the tire. I gave up on finishing the class, and then I made my next mistake: I quit Chuckie Ramo. Initially, I did it because I didn't want to fall or to lift something too heavy there. I was afraid I'd injure myself or the baby. Looking back, however, I know I should have kept working. Jared was never much of a provider.

Jared's mom raised Persian cats, and she was able to get us jobs at the Pendleton Pet Supply Warehouse. The new work seemed to help for a while, and Jared went to some AA meetings while I tried to get counseling. Al-Anon helped me, and I was given a sponsor named Gwen. Al-Anon is a program for codependent people who stay with an addict. Sponsors like Gwen provide encouragement, strength, and prayers as individuals learn how to stop contributing to their loved one's addiction. Gwen helped me see that I had made a habit of bringing strays into my life, hoping they would change their ways if only I loved them enough. "An addict may stick around for a short while," she taught me, "but he will never be yours. He is faithful to his addictions, not to his relationships."

Life with Jared was an ongoing trial. He spent a lot of time at his parents' house playing video games with his little brothers. He also spent hours with his girls and his ex while I waited outside in his car. (I had no idea he was sleeping with his old flame while I sat in the cold.) And if all that weren't trying enough, he had a terrible porn addiction: every weekend, he drove over the state line to stock up on X-rated movies. He'd insist that I watch them with him, but the gross films quickly killed my desire, making me fearful of ever being intimate. I hated them. I wasn't sure how things could get worse, but one day, I came home to find our bedding was stained. "What happened?" I asked.

"The cocker spaniel got sick on the bed, "Jared replied, referring to a dog he'd just rescued from the pound. I scowled at the mess but accepted his story. Later, however, I found one of my nightgowns bearing a similar stain. Soon the truth came out. He'd invited a fifteen-year-old mentally challenged girl into our room. She'd left her innocence in our bed.

While Jared was constantly pushing my tolerance to the limit, he did try to be a gentle and supportive father to Bren, who was wearing glasses by the time he was four. We did have some fun water-gun fights, and we went to the zoo together. Jeb treated Bren like his own and was never cruel or abusive to him. He even took him sledding.

Jeb usually tried to keep his darker side hidden for Bren's sake, so things were often at their worst at night. Jared had a drug habit that demanded that he feed it. One evening, he asked me to give him money so he could replenish his supply. When I refused, he beat my head against the brick wall of our living room. This was nothing new. He often kicked me and knocked me around if I failed to give him money for drugs. His temper was terrifying, but I was so glad he didn't hurt the baby that I tried not to focus on how he made me feel.

I had applied for Section 8 housing, hoping to put some distance between us, but I'd not heard anything about my application yet. Mom's house was not an option, and I had nowhere else to go. For a while, I considered returning to Benjamin, but I had discovered that he was about to marry. I felt I had no one and found that his complete rejection of me stung.

I didn't have much for the new baby and hoped to secure some help from Jared's mom and dad. I knew they were generally nice folks who were financially secure. Just months before, Jared's dad had bought him an expensive white sports car. Jeb would sit in it, smoking his dope and cigarettes, while I struggled to keep up with Bren as our new baby blossomed inside me. It broke my heart when Jared beat me to the punch in asking them for help with the baby. They gave him cash, and Jeb blew it all on drugs.

On August 17, 1987, Ethan was born at U Hospital. I made sure his initials spelled J. E. B.—a tradition in Jared's family. For twelve hours, I labored to deliver a baby who was two weeks late. (In later years, I'd joke that Ethan was probably behind schedule because he was busy trying to argue his way out of being born.) I gazed into Ethan's tiny face and smiled. He looked like a little old, bald man. From the second I heard his cry, I knew he'd be strong-willed.

I had not spent much time preparing Bren for the coming of his half brother. I should have reassured him that my love for him would remain just as strong even as my love multiplied to extend to his little sibling. Bren resented Ethan from day one. It was sad to see the spirit of jealousy and selfishness descending on his little face. In retrospect, I'm sure it was partly my fault that he so resented Ethan's intrusion. I treated Bren like an adult, and I talked to him as one, often enlisting his help. I was tough on him, not allowing him to be a child. That fact grieves me to this day.

My new housing arrangements came through, but some of the excitement over that news faded when Jared decided to come with us to the little yellow house with the single tree in the backyard. I quickly saw that he had no patience for life with a newborn. Something about it seemed to clash with his bipolar disorder, bringing out his worst. Little things like my pausing in the day to clean out the infant's tiny nose would make him have a fit and tell me to go somewhere else to take care of it. Even more frustrating, Ethan's constant cries for attention made Jared rage. "Shut him up right now!" At night I'd hold the baby to my chest, bouncing him and singing until he'd drift to sleep. After that, I'd curl up in Rani's bed, which was empty since she so rarely visited. I'd get a little rest before Ethan would wake up again, screaming. For nine months, I offered him nothing but my own milk. We had so little food.

One evening, I sat in a recliner chair, nursing Ethan. Jared wanted me to get high with him, and I turned him down. Immediately, he got so angry that he flipped Ethan and me backward in the chair. We landed on the heater: I thank God it was not on. Scrambling to my feet and holding my screaming baby close, I managed to get out the front door and run across the street to the home of Bren's best friend. I knew she was a Christian woman, and I asked if I could call the police. They arrived and informed me that as long as Jared's belongings were in my house, I didn't have the right to make him leave; it didn't matter that we weren't married.

Several months later, I stood looking out the window. Bren was busily at play, climbing our lone tree and riding his bike without using his hands—apparently relishing in the safety of his training wheels. I knew Ethan's first birthday would arrive soon, and I couldn't wait to move away from Jared.

He'd taken up with a Buddhist cult and had set up a cardboard shrine in our living room; it made the hair on the back of my neck stand up. Add to that the fact that almost daily I was threatened, suffering mental, physical, and emotional abuse, and it's not difficult to grasp why I felt so desperate to leave. But the previous evening, things had reached a climax.Jared had pulled a knife on me and ordered me to stab him.

Though I'd tried to run out the front door or get to the phone, he blocked my path and pulled the phone out from the wall. After that, he took me into the bathroom, effectively containing me with a hail of verbal and physical abuse. I was not only scared of him—I hated him.

In September 1988, the boys and I moved to Tangle Weed Apts. The place was partially furnished, and I loved it. It was close to a grocery store, the hospital, and bus stops. Finally free of Jared's drama, I focused on my little boys.

Ethan was adorable, and he knew it. He always wanted to be the center of attention, and he thrived under praise like, "You're so cute." I decided early on that he was both noble and bighearted. Unfortunately, however, Ethan continued in his strong-willed ways. Dealing with him was not easy.

Bren started school, relieved to find that he only had to wear his glasses until the middle part of that year. His vision had improved. Bren loved to do puzzles, build models, and play with blocks. In no time, he had made several friends. Some, however, were not good influences.

One time the police showed up at my door to say that young Bren and a friend had used the apartment's phone booth to call 911. About that same time, he also began dodging homework assignments, conveniently leaving them in his desk. That started a habit that would prove hard to break.

In those days, I received a very small income that did not stretch very far. We would walk to the bus stop and ride the bus to the store. Once, I got all the way through the checkout line, only to realize I had left my wallet at home! I had to leave the cart there and take the bus home to get the food stamps before I could go back and purchase the food we needed. Another time, I dropped my keys at the bus stop.

Hours passed before I could return to that specific place, and I was delighted to find that my keys still lay in the grass there. I can recount several instances when money was dropped and found or when just the amount of cash I desperately needed would miraculously come to us. God's amazing provision in these situations began to draw my heart back to Him.

9

Searching for My Father and Deceptions along the Way

You will seek the Lord your God, and you will find
Him if you seek Him with all your heart and with
all your soul.

—Deuteronomy 4:29

THROUGHOUT 1988, I tuned in to watch the TBN, and
I heard the teachings of Billy Graham. His words and
the Christian themes portrayed on that channel started
resonated inside my heart. I decided to ask my friend Angie
if she knew of any good Christian churches in the area. She
replied that she attended The Potter's Clay and invited me
to join her there. My U-turn back to the Father had began.

That Sunday, the boys and I attended. I don't think it was a
coincidence that I spent this particular portion of my history
at a church whose name references God as the potter who

shapes us into vessels dedicated to living out His purposes (see Isa. 64:8). In the coming months, as I was washed in the water of God's Word, my mind was cleansed of a lot of wrong thinking. I had a growing desire to live in righteousness.

Not long after we arrived at The Potter's Place, I met Stan, a cab driver and one of the most dedicated servants of God I've ever encountered. My Heavenly Father put "Stan J." in my path to help me to see Christ's involvement in my life and to help me hear and understand His Word so I could teach my children His ways.

Stan J. was an elderly and humble man with a giving heart. He routinely brought prostitutes and addicts into our church, explaining to those who were irritated by his ways that the rejects of society were just the kind of people Jesus loved to help (see Luke 5:29–32; Romans 3:22–23). "Many of us," he'd say, "forget where God found us." With that, he'd head to a pew where he sat with those he'd brought in and treated them well.

Sadly, Stan J. was sometimes persecuted for his devotion to others. A few suggested he was a pervert because he knew where to find prostitutes, bums, and broken people. (He was a cab driver, so it is not too hard to figure out how he found so many hurting people.) One time, someone who wished to rob him held him up at gunpoint; Stan J. reported saying to that thief, "What in the world would you want to do that for?" I'm certain the thug saw the love of Jesus radiating from his eyes when he lowered the gun and left Stan's Cab. Stan J. couldn't so much as recite a scripture without his eyes filling with tears.

Brother Stan had a heart filled with love for our Father, and he became a spiritual dad to me. He was a man of integrity who lived his life to please God. He led a consistent life for Christ, and there was never a doubt in my mind that he loved the Lord. Over the first few months of our acquaintance, Stan J. gave the children and me rides to and from church and took us out to eat at Sizzler. He also hosted us at his home, where my children watched Christian videos. I learned how to distill water and to grow alfalfa sprouts while he gave me advice and encouraged my heart. One time, he even loaned me money to hire a lawyer in the fight to reclaim Rani. (I paid him back, but she remained in the custody of her Aunt Mara.)

Ethan was fifteen months old when I invited my Heavenly Father to come back into my life, asking His forgiveness for having shelved Him in the first place. I so desired to allow Him to lead, shape, mold, and fill me. For the first time, I truly desired that my life would become what He had planned for me. I made a major U-turn, and I was headed in the right direction.

I got involved in the children's ministry, performing skits and teaching Ethan to say, "Praise the Lord." I also decided to stop taking amphetamines, sending back those that I had recently ordered through the mail. And I started making changes to help us have a more godly living space.

When I was told that the pewter wizards and dragons Jared had given me were seen by some as symbols of the demonic and learned that TV could become a portal through which bad language and pornographic images could make their way into my boys' minds, I got rid of them. I went a step further, tossing out anything that had to do with the LDS Church. I had come to see the religion for the twist of truth that it is. (This was no surprise to me since I had first come to realize that during my childhood.)

My only regret from this time in my life is that in my efforts to get on the right track, I'd sometimes go overboard—particularly where sweet Bren was concerned. He was tenderhearted and smart, and he didn't much appreciate it when I made him throw away his Ninja Turtle Frisbee on the notion that God didn't make anything "mutant" and that "sewer turtles must, therefore, be evil." In my defense, I was such a baby Christian in those days that I honestly thought I was protecting him; however, I know that my boy struggled with this new harshness and my inconsistency in living as uprightly as I desired. Still, he was faithful to help me out in the nursery, and I loved to see how good he was at helping the younger children.

It was about this time that the Lord began to teach me spiritual lessons through the various tasks I performed each day. One day as I was cleaning out my fridge, I started thinking about all the wonderful things God had been doing in my life. I considered the twists and turns in my journey to Him. Suddenly, as I chipped away at the ice coating in my freezer, the Lord spoke to my heart.

He told me He chips away at the hard stuff in me just as diligently. Then, as purposefully as I attacked the remaining ice with warm water, I began to understand the importance of daily immersing myself in the water of God's Word. Only when I did that would He be able to reach and remove the tough roots of sin buried deep within me. The longer I waited to give Him access to those deep places in my life, the harder the process of walking right would prove.

Suddenly I felt inspired to sit down and chronicle my story. I got out a pen and some paper and wrote, "A Father's Love for His Daughter." I wanted so much to share with others the grace and love the Father had poured out on me.

Few realize that as sure as the angels in heaven rejoice over a sinner who comes to the Lord (see Luke 15:7), the demons come out to howl when they lose a follower to Team Jesus. Matthew 12:43–45 tells of a person set free of the devil's influence in his life.

The person receives a spiritual makeover of sorts, getting his life cleaned up and set to order. But then, just about the time he's about to enjoy this new freedom, the demon who once dominated his life returns. Only this time, he brings his friends.

While I certainly do not believe the story suggests that Christians can be possessed by devils, I do think it illustrates that the enemy ramps up his assault when people attempt to live as Christ would have them live. If we don't cling to Jesus for the strength we need when that happens, we set ourselves up for failure. We cannot live holy lives without His help.

I had placed my faith in Jesus and was "born again." I had His Holy Spirit at work inside me, and I was learning how to live in a way that pleased Him. I was not, however, immune to temptation. My need to be loved and my codependency issues were still with me, and I'd soon learn that if I gave the devil an inch, he'd be happy to lead me right back into my bad habits. He wanted to re-ice my heart as effectively as God had thawed it.

I met a guy at church whom I will call Dudley. Like me, Dudley was new to the idea of walking in holiness. We both battled the hardest with sexual temptations, and we had eyes for each other.

Aware of our attraction, our kind pastor approached me and warned me not to let myself fall into temptation. Foolishly, I waved off his concern and said, "Pastor, the devil can't tempt me." In taking this "I can handle it myself" approach, I was setting myself up for moral failure.

When I first became aware of the nature of my feelings toward Dudley, I would throw myself on the sanctuary's altar during prayer time. I asked God to heal me and deliver me of the temptation to commit sexual sin. I begged, pleaded, and cried many times. But I also allowed my mind to repeatedly wander into forbidden territory. First Corinthians 10:13 says, "No temptation has overtaken you except such as is common to man; but God *is* faithful, who will not allow you to be tempted beyond what you are able, but with the temptation will also make the way of escape, that you may be able to bear *it*." I chose not to take God's escape route, creeping closer to the edge of disaster until I finally fell.

My relationship with Dudley did not last long. But when I was twenty-five and Easter was just around the corner, we conceived a child. Our baby would grow into an individual just as stubborn as I was when I chose to combat my sin problem on my own rather than relying on the Lord for help.

"I'm not watching this one," Bren announced upon hearing the news. "I'm going to my friend's house this summer!" He was five years old. Sadly, I truly didn't see that in my selfishness I was neglecting Bren's needs.

For a while, Dudley and I continued to go to The Potter's Clay. I soon knew that he would not be the man I'd marry, and I started to feel anxious over my sons' need for a father. It occurred to me that the new baby might be yet another son. It grieved me to think I could have three little boys without a man to guide them.

I spent some time with Mom just before the baby was due. She'd recently been through some major changes, and I found her more agreeable than in our past encounters. My labor had to be induced, and still it seemed my newest child was in no hurry to arrive.

In my imagination, I can picture the little one stubbornly refusing to come out on the day scheduled for his arrival, already sensing my initial rejection over the issue of his gender. To this day, I believe God had a talk with my baby in those hours leading up to delivery. "You are important to her," He surely said. "You will be loved deeply. You will be by her side more than any other."

Perhaps stirred by this blessing from His Heavenly Father, Daniel finally made his appearance. But I was so disappointed that he wasn't a girl, I cried. I deeply regret that my precious son may have sometimes noticed my disappointment throughout his young life.

I loved him desperately, and I would never exchange him, but I was so sad I couldn't offer him the dad I knew he needed. Stubborn and observant little Daniel had a wrinkled face that looked so sad. The expression and his brown eyes pierced my heart. "Daniel," I admitted when we had a moment alone, "I don't know how I'm going to manage. But then again, I can do all things through God who gives me strength."

Though my children were not exactly planned, they are each precious gifts. Not only did God warm my heart through their sticky kisses, cuddly little hugs, and their sweet voices, but He also used them to teach me so much. It wasn't easy being a single parent, and I learned that my children would observe and often follow my lead.

When I did things that compromised my values, they witnessed the fallout. Anytime I chose to live in a way contrary to God's Word, I suffered the consequences. Worse, my children lost a little more respect for my authority and grew unsure about just how much value there is in a relationship with the Father.

Sometimes I'd cry as I watched their struggles, my heart broken over seeing my babies wallow in stubborn ignorance and rebellion. It made me wonder how often the Father watches each of His children stumble down life's path, often trying to make it without Him. God taught me through those times that I must learn to parent as He does: patience, love, and prayer are my best tools.

God never gives up on His children, and His mercies are new every morning. I needed to learn how to discipline my growing babies in a way that would turn their hearts toward God. I had to learn to say, "I'm sorry," and to be there for them, offering forgiveness and a hug when they repentantly admitted their need for help. No matter how frustrating I found their choices, I could not give up on my babies. God never gives up on His.

I stayed in the Tangle Weed Apartments until my lease ended; after that, we moved to western part of Jordon City, where we had a larger apartment with a huge living area, a nice kitchen, and two bathrooms. Bren and Ethan shared a bedroom, and I kept Daniel's crib in our spacious laundry room. Dudley kept the baby on Sundays, and I picked him up at the evening service.

By this time, Ethan was about three and becoming increasingly testy and difficult. I was horrified when he told me one day that he was going to get a gun and shoot me so an ambulance would come and take me away. Bren, then seven, had a pet gerbil. Ethan pulled the poor thing's tail and it ran for cover. I do not think we ever caught it. Ethan was always keeping me on my toesDaniel was in a walker by the time he was six months old. Every chance he got, he'd wheel himself into the bathroom and pull all the toilet paper off the roll—just as Bren had done at that age. He was also quick to pull all the *Dr. Seuss* and *Help Me Be Good* books off the shelf, and he would fill his mouth with things like soap, crayons, or dirt the second my back was turned. I used to marvel that he could be such a quiet, stubborn little boy at such a tender age. He was an observer from the start, and I often wondered what was going through his mind as he watched his older brothers.

I loved taking pictures of the boys making goofy expressions as they laughed and played or worked their lathered hair into shampoo Mohawks in the tub. The many joys of being their mom outweighed the sorrows of parenting alone. We loved water-gun fights, hide-and-seek, Trouble, building blocks, and doing puzzles.

I decided during this time that I needed to seek godly counsel on raising them to be little men. Some of the best advice I received—some of it came too late to do the good it might have achieved had I used it earlier—taught me that identity needs to be instilled within a child at a young age. A parent can play an important role in helping to build a spiritual understanding of who God is and how we can reach out to Him by putting faith in His Son. Children need to learn to establish their own personal relationship with the Father. They must recognize they can rely on Him for help, even when grown-ups fail them.

Parents also have the opportunity to help guide children toward their God-given destiny and purpose. We see what talents, gifts, and interests they have and then work to build them up toward reaching their goals. Further, we must recognize that we cannot do everything for them. Our job is to prepare them so that by the time they are adults, they will default to seeking God for themselves and for their children.

The overarching goal for parents, then, is to love our growing babies as God loves them. Bearing their pain so we might best know how to apply God's Word in their lives that will bring hope, healing and understanding to the situations. To offer a soft answer that draws them closer to knowing the Father's love. To touch with gentleness that His anointing might flow through our hands to heal, restore, uplift, and to edify our little ones—even when they aren't so little anymore.

It was about August of 1990 when Dudley gave me my first bible. I pored over its words and applied its teaching until the pages came loose. And while I found it increasingly embarrassing to go back to The Potters Clay after my indiscretion, I started to bring some "church" home. David Wilkerson's messages came in the mail monthly and ministered to me greatly (David Wilkerson was the

Founding Pastor of Times Square Church in New York City. He was called to New York in 1958 to minister to gang members and drug addicts.) For many years, he would remain my teacher as Saint John continued to minister to me and my family as well.

My greatest pleasure was being involved with my children, and I knew their playmates within the complex could use some positive influence. I began holding Bible studies for the younger children in our neighborhood and sometimes invited any child who wanted to ask Christ into his or her heart to take that step. One mother in particular challenged my call to witness to her son. I replied with Luke 18:16.

Jesus called the young ones to Him and said, "Let the little children come to Me, and do not forbid them; for of such is the kingdom of God." I talked with the boys and told them I hoped to see them in heaven someday.

There are many boys growing up without a father to guide them and correct them. Just as much as little girls not having a mother to comfort, soothe, and nurture.

We need to bring hope, healing, peace, and unconditional love to a hurting generation of lost children and youth. Charles Stanley put it this way: "The worst kind of rejection for a daughter is the rejection of her daddy." And if a boy doesn't respect his mother, he won't respect anyone in authority—especially a woman.

Boys learn how to be God fearing, tenderhearted, and respectful and learn to love and achieve with a father influencing and modeling the same.

God will never leave you empty.
He will replace everything you have lost.
If He asks you to put something down,
It's because He wants you to pick up
Something greater.

10

The Wiles of the Devil

Put on the whole armor of God, that you may be
able to stand against the wiles of the devil.

—Ephesians 6:11

I DECIDED I needed to find my biological father. I wanted
to tell him about my new faith. I really wanted my dad
to be a part of my boys' lives, and a part of me continued
to hope for his affirmation and affection. Years had passed
since I'd seen him, though, and I wasn't even certain where
he lived. In those days before the Internet, tracking a
person was no easy task. I was delighted when I discovered
he had relocated to North Carolina. Finally, I could speak
with him!

Cheered by this reconnection, I decided to stand and
share my testimony at church. Soon I would no longer
attend The Potter's Clay; instead, I would be gathering

with a new congregation at Miracle Springs Church. My mother also attended there at that time.

Shortly after that service, a woman named Gidget approached and told me she and her friend Viper wanted to have me over for dinner. Gidget had kept my kids a few times at church, but I did not know her all that well. I certainly didn't know that she had two muscular men, Hobbs and Viper, living with her as roommates.

"You just have to meet my friend Viper," she enthused. "I know you two will really hit it off."

Far less interested in meeting a new man than I was in the promise of eating homemade chicken enchiladas for dinner that evening, I agreed to go.

Dinner turned out to be an interesting affair, and I immediately figured that the two men living with Gidget were drug dealers. The one named Viper, however, seemed a nice-enough guy—even if he did deal. He spoke about church and the Bible, and he quickly became friends with my oldest son, Bren Ashton.

Viper was an African American—the only black man I had ever dated. Though he was ten years older than I was, and I wasn't particularly attracted to him, I was charmed by the way he related to my son Bren. They went on fun adventures together. Viper and I went out a few times, and I wasn't terribly surprised the day he asked me to marry him.

I may not have taken the offer seriously, however, had it not been for his claim that when he'd first heard me share my testimony in our church, God had given him a vision that I was to be his wife. Now, I certainly had not witnessed or entertained any such visions about him (If a guy is overly friendly with your child or he claims God told him something, run!], but I didn't want to risk somehow disappointing God if Viper had indeed heard from Him. Remember "If in doubt, don't."

I gave the matter serious thought, but it never once occurred to me that Viper was not really a Christian brother but an enemy in disguise. He knew what to say. He knew what to claim. However, he did not truly know Christ. (What disaster I would have avoided had I realized that those who belong to the Lord are known by the fruits of their obedience to Him—not by the fine-sounding claims they make.) Still, in addition to my suspicion that Viper continued to deal, I had to overcome two concerns before I could seriously consider joining my life with his. First, I wasn't sure whether it was biblically appropriate for people of two different ethnicities to marry.

This concern comes up often. The Bible, however, is wholeheartedly against this misunderstanding. Genesis 3:20 declares Eve the mother of *all* the nations. Acts 17:26 states, "And [God] has made from one blood every nation of men to dwell on all the face of the earth." Each of us is a direct descendant of Adam and Eve, made in the image of God. Regardless of what Darwin taught in *On the Origin of Species*, God's Word is clear that we are one race: the human race. The color differences we see are in reality just minor genetic variations.

I did have some doubts about the depth of Viper's Christian commitment and had a hard time dismissing them. I knew 1 Timothy 4:14 teaches that we must not be unequally yoked with unbelievers, but Viper *claimed* to be a believer, so I wasn't sure the passage made a good argument against him. I decided to ask some other believers for guidance.

I talked to Stan J. about the situation, and he said I would know what I should do. I wanted him to tell me that marrying Viper was a bad idea, but Brother Stan wanted me to figure that out for myself. He never judged me or criticized me.

I wanted an answer from God so desperately. Many answers had come previously from one of David Wilkerson's messages I received in the mail. I would send a seed offering or tithe and pray for God to give me a special word through Wilkerson's ministry. The Lord was faithful to answer my prayers, even using the minister's weekly messages to give me just the guidance and encouragement I needed.

On this particular occasion, the Pastor Wilkerson sent this scripture: "It is better to trust in the Lord than to put confidence in man" (Ps. 118:8–9). The advice was welcomed, and I did mull over it. In the end, however, I chose to trust that Viper was the man God intended for me.

Viper and I married at the courthouse on September 18, 1990. I remember that I felt nauseated during the little ceremony as Stan and Gidget stood as witnesses. Looking back, I wonder whether the Holy Spirit was making one last attempt to warn me against the coming danger.

Immediately following the wedding, we went back to my apartment. As soon as we stepped over the threshold, Viper began his mission to use me and to play me for a fool. When I refused some of the things he suggested doing in our bedroom, he called me a "goody Christian woman." He didn't care in the slightest that years of taking sexual abuse from Oscar and Jared had taken their toll.

Instead, he called me a cuss word. Horrified by the radical change in his behavior, I called him one back. I ended up spending our wedding night in the tub with the bathroom door locked. In my hand, I held a knife, and I toyed with the idea of ending my life right there. How could I once again fall for such a cruel and uncompassionate man?

The next day, Gidget returned the boys home. Viper "welcomed" them by demanding that Bren give him back the hat and another item he had once given him as gifts. It broke my heart to see the look of confusion on Bren's young face. I think in that moment he realized Viper had played him to get to me.

In the coming months, Viper played havoc on our lives. He didn't have a job. Rather than going out to find one, he let me use up all my money feeding him and paying his bills. Since I had married, my welfare checks stopped coming and my subsidized housing help went away too.

Things began to get tight, and I increasingly disliked him. Viper was cruel and demanding, even calling my boys names. When I learned that he had not paid a penny of taxes in years, I finally concluded that he'd married me simply to use my boys and me as tax deductions. It soon became clear that he loved meth—an addiction I'd known nothing about prior to our marriage—far more than he would ever love a family.

Viper had a habit of biting his lip when he was upset. I became fearful of the gesture because I knew what it meant. Still, I'm not sure that I feared his anger as much as I hated the mind games he played with me. I recall that he'd tell me to make him a peanut butter sandwich. I'd obey his command and present the sandwich only to have him yell at me and ask me why I kept making him peanut butter sandwiches. Didn't I know he hated them? Other times he would taunt me. He'd tell me he was going to lock me up in the mental institution and take my boys from me.

When I tried to defend myself and told him to keep his hands off my boys, he said that my actions were further proof that I was unstable. How I felt like his prisoner! It didn't help that I knew the man's hands were registered as weapons.

I mentioned that Viper knew a lot about God and even attended church occasionally, but after only a few days of marriage to him, I knew beyond a doubt that Jesus was not in that man's heart.

Not only did he have a complete lack of respect for the Lord in his own life, but he also set out to undermine both my authority and any spiritual teaching I gave the boys.

One time I sat down with the kids to pray, and little Ethan began by blessing the couch, floor, and door. I loved hearing his little voice and admired his easy acceptance of the Lord, and I chuckled because he was just so cute. Viper immediately broke into our prayer time and scolded me for laughing; he told me to leave if I was going to be disrespectful.

The boys stared at me as Viper continued to tear me down. "This was wrong, wasn't it, guys?" he asked. They looked at me and then back at him before nodding. My heart broke as I saw him turning their little hearts against me. In the years to follow, my little guys would come to routinely disrespect both me and any other woman in authority.

Not long into our marriage, Viper decided to go to school for his CDL license. Not only was the training out of state, but it also lasted six to eight weeks. My money was gone, and I knew I'd need a way to pay the rent. I asked

Viper to send me some money when he got settled. He sent only fifty dollars, and I knew when I saw that cash that there was no way I'd avoid eviction. I'd need that little bit of money just to put food in our mouths.

I spoke to Viper on the phone and told him that he'd left me with no choice. Since I had no way to pay the bills, the boys and I would have to sell what we could and go down to Ava, Missouri, where my dad then lived. (He'd moved on from North Carolina.) Viper didn't care a bit what happened to us or to our things. He just made a quick stop by the apartment to pick up his own belongings before going right back to school.

I was left to move the kids and me across country on almost no money. Thankfully, Judy, a friend I had met at The Potter's Clay, came to help me sell my things. Judy was a beautiful and loving mother who wanted a more intimate relationship with our Father and desired only the best for her son, Allen. She encouraged me and made that moment in my life a lot less lonely. I think we ministered to each other that evening.

The children and I took a bus to my dad's. It wasn't by any means a pleasure trip. Though my kids were small and I had no adult traveling companion to help corral them, I found that I had to practically demand that people move so my boys could sit by me. To make the trip even more difficult, Daniel had to sit on my lap. Only when he filled his diaper with diarrhea could I convince the bus driver to stop so I could get him cleaned up. The stops also gave the boys a chance to stretch their restless limbs.

We traveled on that bus for three long days. Finally, we made it to Ava, where Dad picked us up in his green station wagon. He took us to the little two-bedroom house he and his wife shared; I remember that they used propane for cooking and heating. I was delighted to see that Dad had built a closet for me as he waited for our arrival; I appreciated that gift more than I can say.

I rather liked the small town where Dad lived. His house was within walking distance of the elementary school, and I seriously thought about living there permanently. It helped that I had a friend across the street. Delta was a sweet elderly lady who would always say, "Ya doin' all right?" She'd let me use her telephone regularly, and I would give her money for her phone bill. (I had a little cash left from the belongings I'd sold to make the trip.) Unfortunately, things weren't going so well at Dad's house. In those days, the man had quite a temper, and I think it was hard on him to have four extra people—three of them being busy little boys—in his small home. He tried to put up a child's gate between our room and the rest of the house, but I felt that he was essentially creating a cage for my baby. In retrospect, I understand that his intent was not to treat him as an animal.

Daniel was just starting to cruise, and Dad was trying to keep him safe. Still, I became upset and we argued. In the weeks that followed, Dad began insisting on his right to discipline my boys. Things escalated, and I caught him about to knock three-year-old Ethan off the kitchen chair with a harsh pop to the mouth.

I called the police. I was terrified of any man being angry and threatening violence; this was all I knew to do at the time.

but they would not do anything to help cool Dad's temper. In the end, my call only caused Dad to get more easily upset with us because I had embarrassed him. And in time, I'd figure out that part of his anger and frustration stemmed from the fact that his white daughter was married to a black man. That detail so irritated him that he didn't seem to care how Viper treated me.

One day, Viper showed up, and he and Dad had a nice long talk. They didn't realize that through the wall I could hear every word they said as I sat in the bedroom.

"Look, I don't want her with me," Viper said, as if I were a piece of extra luggage he didn't want to carry.

"Well, I don't want her here either!" Dad replied, clearly ready for the man to take his wife and kids off his hands. "*Take her with you.*"

This was followed by a string of mean names for me, and every one broke another piece out of my battered heart. As I sat caged in our room, I felt the children and I were not wanted. And finally, hoping Dad might soften toward his grandkids with me out of the way, I gave Dad and my stepmother permission to take care of the boys, turning over the right to cash my assistance checks as well as access to the food stamps I counted on to keep us fed. Then I joined Viper for a long haul in his eighteen-wheeler. At the time, I felt I had no other choice.

I didn't like being on the road, showering in truck stops and traveling with Viper—who of course insisted on his husbandly rights. Living in that truck with him felt like being in prison. But the worst part of that time was the separation from my boys. Though I'd given Dad and his wife six hundred dollars in assistance to buy them much-needed clothes and vitamins, I couldn't stop wishing I could be there to provide for them in person.

The ache was magnified by the fact that Viper provided me with nothing. I don't know where the cash he made as a trucker went. He certainly never spent it on the children or me.

Finally, Viper allowed me to call Dad's house while he sat in his truck, waiting impatiently. He didn't care how much I wanted to be with my boys. I don't think he even wanted to hear about them. If I was upset before my talk with Bren and Ethan, I was a wreck by the time I hung up the phone.

Through tears, my kids reported that they were scared of the intense Missouri tornado and thunderstorms and that my dad had used the whole check I'd given to clothe and nourish them on having his car repaired! I immediately began to cry over this news and just knew I had to get back to my children as soon as possible.

When I tried to tell Viper what was happening, the man told me to quit crying and suck it up. He was completely unsympathetic and clearly did not care about the four people who made up his family.

"We have to travel a steep grade up ahead," he said as I tried to pull myself together. "One of the brakes is out, so it could be a wild ride."

The night was turning stormy, and I was emotionally spent. I lay behind the cab and prayed.

For two months, I'd endured life on the road with Viper. I'd suffered the humiliation of hearing him tell other truckers that I—his legal wife—was a prostitute he'd picked up. I'd been forced to play endless mind games, each one meant to demean me. And I'd endured sexual encounters that had been anything but loving or gentle.

I was broken down in pieces and by then had such low self-esteem that I neither knew how to stand up to Viper nor had the strength to walk away from him. "If you leave, I will find you," he'd sneer often. "I'll kill you and tell God you simply died."

I hated how he'd adopt the language of my faith or would twist it horribly to humiliate me further. I was genuinely afraid of him.

"Please, Father God," I prayed as Viper maneuvered the truck down the steep grade, "get me home to be with my boys! I will never leave them again."

My prayer was answered that very next morning. Viper literally dumped me off in the middle of nowhere, gave me very little money, and told me to take a bus back to Dad's.

As I set out to make my way home, I was reminded of Psalm 91:1–2, 9–16, a portion of Scripture someone had once sent me in a card.

> He who dwells in the secret place of the Most High Shall abide under the shadow of the Almighty.

> I will say of the Lord, "He is my refuge and my fortress; My God, in Him I will trust."

> Because you have made the Lord, who is my refuge, Even the Most High, your dwelling place, No evil shall befall you, Nor shall any plague come near your dwelling; For He shall give His angels charge over you, To keep you in all your ways.

> In their hands they shall bear you up, Lest you dash your foot against a stone.

> You shall tread upon the lion and the cobra, The young lion and the serpent you shall trample underfoot.

> "Because he has set his love upon Me, therefore I will deliver him; I will set him on high, because he has known My name.

He shall call upon Me, and I will answer him; I will be with him in trouble; I will deliver him and honor him.

With long life I will satisfy him, And show him My salvation."

I knew my life was in a tangle, and I'd brought most of it on myself. Still, I held on to the truth that God loved my boys and me. I would lean on Him. He was my only hope.

I arise today
May the strength of God Pilot us,
May the wisdom of God instruct us,
May the hand of God protect us,
May the word of God direct us,
May the Shield of God Protect us
From snares of devils
From temptation of vices
From everyone who may wish me ill
Afar and near

(Old Irish hymn)

11

Hope in the Darkness

Do not be deceived, God is not mocked; for
whatever a man sows, that he will also reap.

—Galatians 6:7

I ARRIVED BACK at Dad's and immediately began looking at some nearby places where the boys and I could live. As Viper had deserted me beside the interstate, I figured I was free of him and wanted to get my life back on track. It felt like a nightmare when he showed up to ruin my plans.

Viper managed to sucker me into making a bus trip back to Templeville, and I had to pay for it out of my assistance check. The ride on the bus was intense, exhausting, emotional, and stressful. Not only did I have my hands full seeing to the boys' needs, but I also realized I truly had no idea what to expect from Viper anymore. I was frightened by his behavior and was always unsure of his intentions. Still, as I had no one else to whom I could turn, I felt tied to him.

When the bus finally pulled into the station, I gently nudged the kids out into the fresh air and hoped Viper would help me with the bags and perhaps carry Daniel. My arms were tired, and my body ached from that long and uncomfortable ride, but my husband did nothing to help. Instead, he stood by the terminal door with his arms folded, as if waiting for me to catch up to him. As I noted the look on his face, I decided he was the most coldhearted, uncaring, and unfeeling person I had ever known. (Much of his erratic behavior was a direct result of his use of meth, but that was no excuse for the way he treated me.)

Finding we had nowhere else to go, we moved in with Gidget—the woman who had first introduced us to Viper. To this day, I don't completely understand the mysterious relationship between Viper and Gidget. She was in her mid-forties, was generally unconcerned with modesty when at the house, and she would talk at length about her "need" for bodyguards. Living with her was no picnic.

It wasn't long before I realized that Gidget, too, would play mind games with me. She lacked compassion, and her demeanor was sharp and arrogant. Had I not been terrified that Viper would make good on his threat to have me committed if I crossed him, I might have headed back to Dad's house.

One good thing that came from being back in Templeville was that I was closer to my Rani. Sometime in April, a friend mentioned that Rani was at the park. Thrilled with the chance to see my baby girl, who was by then almost nine, I went right over to see her. In the past, her Aunt Mara had worked hard to block our interactions. I hoped she wouldn't be there to interfere this time.

I was surprised to see that both Oscar and Viper were looking on while my daughter played. One of them noticed my approach, and I could tell by the look on his face that the two men were discussing me. I did not like that idea one bit.

Later, Viper bragged that Oscar had told him how he had schemed to take Rani away from me so he would not have to pay child support. On top of all the mental abuse Viper had poured out on me throughout our months together, that little detail of Oscar's betrayal really hurt. I found myself wondering what Viper had told Oscar about me because I knew Viper tried to make me look bad every chance he got.

Without a doubt, the Father was with me that day as my heart thudded with a deeper awareness of the snarls created by my poor choices. I felt so condemned that I created a toxic lemonade of cross tops and crushed caffeine pills and set out to end my life. The attempt failed, only contributing to the esophagus damage I already had. It was both frustrating and reassuring to know that the Lord had foiled my attempt on my life. Though I couldn't see any way out of my situation and though I felt deep guilt over the way my choices had impacted my children, I was sure God loved me despite my acts of disobedience. I knew that He would still help me if only I'd ask.

I lay on the floor, remembering how sweet and innocent Rani had been in those days I'd first brought her home from the hospital. She was mine. I was her mom. And for a short time, all had seemed that it just might work out fine. "Father, please," I asked, "will You please allow me just one more baby? Another chance to mother a little girl?"

Six weeks later, just as June began, I found out I was pregnant. I was excited about the coming of our baby, but I knew the little one was not going to change Viper or the way he treated us. He would no more be the father my new child needed than he was to those I already had. She—I just knew the baby was a girl—would need her Heavenly Father. We all would, and so I continued to pray, to go to church, and to trust God to help me through my mess.

A day came when Viper told me that Gidget's property owner, Thomas Park, had a house for rent. Thomas would take any repairs Viper made to the place off the cost of rent. That sounded like a great plan, though I suspected my husband would make few repairs, and therefore, we'd enjoy little reduction in the rent. When I saw the house, however, I wasn't sure I wanted to move there. The place was a gray fixer-upper built in the 1940s. It had a fence, but I worried over having three little boys living so near a busy street. Still, the school was within walking distance, and there were some other children nearby who were close in age to the kids. I agreed to give the place a try. Frankly, I really didn't have a choice.

We moved in during the first part of August 1991. Unknown to me, Viper began keeping a steady girlfriend about this time. Soon "the snake," as I've since come to think of him, was gone more than he was home. Without furnishings, without cash, without dependable appliances, I was left to build that tumbledown place into a home.

Before I could do that, I needed to secure some form of insurance to cover the baby's arrival. I no longer qualified for financial aid or Medicaid since I had married Viper. When I became pregnant, however, I learned that the baby was qualified for the "Baby Your Baby" program. I immediately applied for that help and was so blessed to receive it.

The next matter to tackle was finding a washer and dryer. Running our huge piles of laundry to the Laundromat wouldn't have been a big deal had I a car and the driver's license I'd never gotten. As it was, I had a tough time keeping up with the laundry. I started to pray about what I could do about that and Brother Saint John came to mind. Sweet, faithful Saint John chose to help meet this need. Each week, he would come to get our laundry and would return it clean and folded! In time, Catholic Community Charities provided us with a used washer and dryer. This too was a gift from my Heavenly Father.

For a while, I wondered what to do about furnishings. I did not own a bed, nor did the children have beds or dressers. After sleeping on the floor for several months, I started ramping up my prayers that the Lord would provide for us in this matter too.

When Viper was home, he was nice to Rani (who sometimes visited), and he was fairly pleasant to Daniel. To my precious Ethan and Bren, on the other hand, he could be brutally mean. For Ethan's fourth birthday, I planned a backyard barbeque. I invited Susanna and the neighbors. As the party wound to a close, Viper said he wanted me to go buy him some beer. As I was still hosting and hated to buy him alcohol, I suggested that he go get it himself. I had determined not to buy poison for people, and he knew that.

Moments later, as I was saying good-bye to my sister, I heard Ethan screaming inside the house. As I threw open the door to see what was wrong, I could hear the unmistakable slap of a belt hitting flesh. Chills ran down my spine, and my heart pounded at the sound of my son being beaten. I felt physically sick when I turned into the bathroom to find Ethan standing in the tub. Ugly red-and-white welts were all over his back. Viper had vented his anger at me on my helpless baby!

As I tried to soothe Ethan, I knew I had to find a way to get Viper locked up. I decided to fill out a police report on Viper's abuse of my boys. While it would take me a little while to find the courage to follow through with that plan, I didn't waste the in-between time. I continued to hold on to my Father's hand, trusting Him to pull me through and to work all my bad choices out for our good somehow.

I got more involved at church (I had begun going to Miracle Springs). I was about four or five months pregnant when I met Ronan and Grace Wallace. They were planning to start up their own church and wanted me to go with them.

Ronan and Grace taught me to pray like a true spiritual warrior. They took me under their wings and taught me biblical principles and how to apply them. They compared the journey of spiritual growth to the physical training an athlete endures, and something about that made a lot of sense to me. They accepted me as their daughter and loved my children.

Throughout that very difficult season of our lives, they came to my house two or three times a week, studied with me in my home, gave me rides to and from church, and generally shepherded me in my faith. I could see through their actions that the pair truly loved me, and I soaked up not only what they taught me about spiritual warfare but also what they shared about how to conduct my life as the Lord commands in His Word.

Together, Ronan, Grace, and I made a covenant with God to begin praying hard over Viper. They counseled me on how to save my marriage, believing that God could indeed redeem my husband. They even tried to talk to and pray with Viper when he appeared at the house. After some prayer services, I would slip anointed prayer cloths under my husband's pillow. I began praying over him as he slept.

Though Viper continued to dabble in meth, I could feel the atmosphere of prayer in the home. It was a tangible reminder that my Father was with me in the storm.

12

Naomi

> But You have seen, for You observe trouble and grief, To repay it by Your hand. The helpless commits himself to You; You are the helper of the fatherless.
>
> —Psalm 10:14

IF NOT FOR my hope that sharing my story might somehow help other young women avoid joining their lives with men like my husband, Viper, I would not disclose much of the drama that unfolded over the course of our marriage. In retrospect, the only bright spot in my relationship with him was the precious child we had together. Still, Viper was a cruel and mean man—not just to me but toward my precious babies. (He even *insisted* that I eat tuna and shellfish throughout my pregnancy.)

Though I repeatedly tried to block his access to us, he'd manipulate his way around restraining orders and would reappear despite promises to stay away when the kids and I would return from stints in a shelter home. Each attempt I made to regain freedom was defeated by his manipulations. As much as it breaks my heart to admit it, that con artist gave my kids and me little choice but to live in the shadow of his abuse.

I recall one day when Bren was playing with his fire truck. Viper told him to put it up, and Bren turned around to drive it into his bedroom. Viper interpreted this as disrespect and grabbed the seven-year-old, bashing his head into the wall and making a huge hole in the drywall. It all happened so fast there was little I could do, but when I went to comfort Bren, Viper told me if I took one step closer, I was going to get it. I had no doubt he meant what he said.

When it was safe to do so, I went to the neighbors to call the police. I also called my mom and asked her to come get the boys while I went about getting a restraining order. In the end, not so much because of his actions toward my son but because of an outstanding warrant, Viper was arrested that night.

I couldn't believe it when Ronan paid my husband's $800 bail and brought Viper home. While the man was likely somewhat duped by the misunderstanding that Viper was merely a struggling Christian and surely didn't grasp the extent of what was really going on behind our walls, I was so upset and scared to see my husband coming through our door that I felt angry at my friend. Even he could not see that Viper was a con artist and an abuser of the worst sort! Maybe he did he see and didn't care? The minister was African American also.

The restraining order failed to materialize, and I welcomed the boys home the next morning with a heavy heart. In the coming months, Viper repeatedly forced himself on me—once even in the presence of my kids. That time I fought him with everything I had.

When I got up, I managed to push the coming baby's crib between us and put a small hole in the wall in the process. He took advantage of the opportunity to grab my unguarded social security card and identification so he could get copies of them. Angry and helpless over all he was putting us through and terrified he would use my ID to wreak more havoc for us, I panicked. The second I could get out of the room, I called the police. When they arrived, Viper ran out to talk with them. He blamed the whole ugly scene on me!

"Ma'am," the officer said to me, "you'll either have to leave, or I'll have to take you to the station."

Rather than pointing out what had really happened and drawing attention to the fact that Viper's hands— not mine—were registered as weapons, I called a friend to take the boys and me into her home. Later, I gathered the children, whom I couldn't bear to leave with Viper, and went to stay at the YWCA, which housed a battered women's shelter. After a time, Viper agreed to let me come back to the house and promised he would leave me alone. I shouldn't have believed him.

In the coming months, my husband would play mental games with me, refusing to go to church with me or even to let me take the boys. Meanwhile, I did what I could to be a good parent to my children.

Leaned on Ronan and Grace for ongoing spiritual guidance, and I valued their advice. (I forgave Ronan for bringing Viper home from jail, and I trusted that he and his wife—who made it clear she had nothing to do with his bailing out Viper—really did want the best for us.) Rani would visit often during that period, and I loved having her close. It was such a blessing to see her make Christmas things for her siblings. She created personalized pillows and banks.

Both she and Bren painted ceramics, played with Play Doh, and helped me out with the children at church. Despite all the chaos Viper managed to cause in those hard days, the kids and I made some grand memories together.

Of course, not all moments in parenting are fun and lighthearted. I had a hard time with Ethan and Bren, who were certainly not above misbehaving as little boys do. But as I found that time-outs were not always effective.

It hurt my hand to spank them, so I made a wooden paddle to use on their bottoms when a stern talking to wasn't enough to change their behavior. While Viper accused me of being terrible for creating such a thing and even turned me into DHS when I used it on Bren, my intent was never to injure my children.

Scripture talks about how in sparing the rod of correction we spoil our children, effectively teaching them not to respect authority (see Prov. 13:24). I spanked the boys for one reason: I honestly wanted to teach them right from wrong. While I admit I did sometimes discipline in anger, I was never cruel.

Though my temper constantly fought against my best efforts, I did long to be as kind and understanding with my kids as my Heavenly Father was toward me. It was so important to me for my children to feel loved, protected, and secure. Viper constantly worked against me on that. The fact that I sometimes failed to stay rooted in the Word didn't help our discipline situation.

Others, however, helped me build security and love for my little family. I continue to thank God for the many ways His people stepped up to help us! Saint John and a woman named GG provided us with food, sometimes leaving surprise groceries on our porch. Saint John made a habit of giving us rides to the store and to doctors' appointments, too.

Then one day, there came a knock at my door. I opened it to find strangers standing outside, asking me if I needed a California king-sized bed. Thrilled that the Lord had decided to answer my prayer for a comfortable place to sleep, I praised God! I soon found some king-sized sheets from a charity place that covered my need for linens. And not long after that, a group of people who subbed for Santa asked me to fill out an application outlining the needs and wants of the children.

That Christmas we received holiday food, and the children got bunk beds, a dresser, homemade matching quilts, and big Klondike stockings filled with toys and clothes. I even remember putting together Big Wheels for them! And if all that were not blessing enough, I received some winter boots for myself. I wore them for the next twelve years.

Deep in my heart, I knew I had to find a way to rid myself of Viper, who was often gone for long periods of time anyway. One day, I came across 1 Corinthians 7:15: "If the unbeliever departs [a marriage], let him depart; a brother or a sister is not under bondage in such *cases*." In that moment, I decided that if Viper were to leave me permanently on his own accord, I'd no longer be bound by our marriage vows. But how would I convince the con to leave?

I decided to ramp up my prayers for deliverance from Viper. On a few occasions, I attended all-night prayer meetings at Miracle Springs Church, asking God's blessings over my home and children. Then every night for two weeks, I would get up and pray for two hours at a time just as I had agreed to do in a covenant I'd made with

Ronan and Grace. I know that God saw the desperation of my heart.

"You have to love your husband, Shamara," Ronan advised me.

"I can't tolerate him," I confessed. But then I asked God to give me a love for Viper, and I was shocked to find that He did just that. I was never in love with my husband, but God did give me a measure of love, of compassion, for him.

After about two weeks, I could see that the Christian love I offered Viper began to bother him. He could not understand how I could offer him loving kindness after he was so terribly cruel to me. Meanwhile, I drew closer to the Lord, taking the words of the song "Lord Prepare Me to be a Sanctuary" to heart. I had to sing that tune as a solo at church one day, and while I'm sure I only made a joyful noise unto the Lord since I am not a gifted singer, the lyrics lifted my spirit and gave me new strength for the journey.

March 30, 1992, arrived and GG watched the boys for me so I could go to the hospital to deliver my baby girl. I smiled as my little guys waved good-bye to me. Unlike times past when I blindly trusted my sons to the care of someone unworthy, I knew that this time I was leaving them in excellent care. GG was a prayer warrior and a wise woman. She genuinely loved my children, and they loved her.

Baby Naomi was positioned bottom first—just as I was at my own delivery. I'm sure lil Naomi was afraid of being born into a home of chaos. Just as I came out backward and doing things the hard way, so did she have to be forced from the save haven of my womb and presence of the Father.

I had to have a C-section and asked the doctor to cut my tubes before he stitched me closed. I kissed Naomi's beautiful little face and felt my heart swell with love for her. I saw my precious daughter as a gift from God, and I could not wait to show her to her siblings. Having to present her to Viper was the only damper on my day. As I watched him hold her, I was so afraid he would find a way to take her from me. *Fear will run your life if you let it*, I coached myself as I dressed Naomi for the trip home. *Faith and fear are not compatible.* I've got to choose to live and to speak in faith.

I arrived at home to see that GG had purchased some things for the new baby, and the boys were indeed happy to have a baby sister. The excitement of the day abruptly ended, however, when my dear friend told me Ethan had been talking about a bad man touching him.

She asked me if I knew anything about that, and I was devastated to realize my son had been abused in a manner I'd never imagined. Deeply concerned, I asked four-year-old Ethan to talk to me, but he made up a random story to cover the truth. I did not want to confront Viper out of concern that he would hurt Ethan worse for saying something about this latest form of abuse, but I knew that big changes were needed in our family.

A few days later, I thought I found the answer when Viper ordered me to divorce him, but no sooner had I digested this news than Viper explained that the situation would only last a few weeks before we would remarry on Mother's Day. To this moment, I have no idea why Viper made this ridiculous decision, but I do know why I didn't fight him harder on the "remarry" part.

First, I had just had three wisdom teeth pulled and was in so much pain that I couldn't think clearly.

Second, I had so allowed my dad's attitude toward my relationship with a black man to pollute my thinking that I began to fear I'd never find a man who would accept all my children.

And third—and I realize this is a terribly weak reason—I felt ashamed to think I couldn't make my marriage succeed.

I wanted Viper either to miraculously change or to disappear completely from our lives on his own accord. Though Ronan and Grace discouraged the remarriage idea and my pastor refused to officiate, the thought of what Viper might do if I refused to remarry him made me shiver. I did not want to lose Naomi as I had Rani! (Fear of losing Naomi, wanting my boys away from abuse, and being faithful to my God made my choices difficult.)

I went along with Viper's plan, continuing to pray for his salvation and focusing my energy on my little ones. I had dedicated my older children to the Lord at The Potter's

Clay church, and I dedicated Naomi to the Lord at Miracle Springs Church. As I watched the pastor take her in his arms, I smiled at the truth that she was both beautiful and precious to me. She was my sunshine in the darkest of times.

Her baby smile and laughter were things we all needed as we navigated the storms of Viper's mood swings. The boys were so protective of her that it warmed my heart. (I not only committed her to the Lord that day but committed to being her protector and teacher and to rear her to fear God and not find men like her dad, the viper).

Sadly, round two of marriage to Viper failed to go any better than round one. Bren told me that one day "that Viper" had taken him to Pioneer Transit Park, where they picked up a "Forty Tina," a term that refers to how much meth a person buys.

Another time I came into the room to see that Viper had put Ethan in the corner with a mouth full of hot peppers, insisting that he not swallow and that he stand with his arms straight out. I was so upset when Ethan started to gag and throw up but that cruel, venomous snake made him stay there a moment more until he finally let me intervene.

How much my children and I could have been spared had I left that man at the first sign of abuse! I blame myself that I allowed fear of what *might* happen to keep us entrapped in the nightmare of what *was* happening. I didn't have anyone to help the boys and me escape. My children deserved a better home than that.

Momentary relief came when Viper went back to hauling freight out of state. We enjoyed relative peace while he was away, though he would sometimes stop by with yogurt for the family before delivering me bad news. On one such occasion, he stopped in to tell me he had slept with a woman who had AIDS. Supposedly, he'd been taking care of her for a few months and that was why I hadn't heard from him for so long. After he left, I had to go several times to be checked for AIDS. Thankfully, God spared me that. I was not, however, spared this new worry my husband had brought home.

In the weeks that followed, Viper would occasionally drop by our home when he was higher than a kite. Sweat poured profusely down his face, and at times, he would literally shake. Meth, that demon drug, was gaining more and more control over him.

"God," I prayed, "please deliver us from this situation. Father, please protect my precious Naomi. Don't let him take off with her."

Things came to a head one day when Viper warned me I could no longer go to church. "If you go," he hissed, "I'll kill you."

"If I go to church, I will worship the Lord there," I replied with a boldness and calm that had to have come from the Holy Spirit. "If I die, I go to the Lord."

Completely incensed by this, Viper tried to strangle life out of me.

For a moment, panic rose. I knew he could end my life. But then it occurred to me that Viper, strong as he was, was weak compared with my Father. My husband was bound by the devil, but that didn't mean he would win this battle between us. The enemy has a major weakness: he fears the power of Christ.

Carefully drawing air as I was able, I used my exhales to hum. I hummed, "Oh the Blood of Jesus," as loudly as I could while Viper yelled at me to shut up. "I will kill you," he threatened. I kept on humming and managed to raise my hands to my husband's chest. Distracted by the gentle touch, Viper slightly eased his grip on my throat.

"In the name of Jesus, I command you to loose me," I said softly, and just like that, Viper fell down—unconscious as a rock—because of the intervention of the Spirit of God.

"Bren!" I yelled. "Bren, go get Ronan."

My son took one look at Viper's prone form, jumped out the window, and ran for help.

In the moments while I waited for my pastor to arrive, Viper woke. I was immediately alarmed by the change that had come to his face. His eyes were huge and dark. Though Viper's face and form were the same as ever, I got the distinct impression that it was not my husband staring back at me.

"Who—who are you?" I stammered.

"I'm Death," it answered, "and I am going to kill him."

Apparently possessed by whatever evil he had so long embraced, Viper went out the door, got on a ten-speed, and rode by the house on his way down the street. I'll never forget the long, creepy stare he gave me as I watched him leave.

"Jesus, help him," I prayed.

Ronan soon arrived, and I told him what had happened. After that, I decided to kick Viper out of the house for good. That, of course, did not go as smoothly as I'd hoped. He soon arrived with a stack of electronics he had taken from some store and yelled, "Let Daddy in!" When I refused, he decided to camp out in the yard. He then went about washing his body in the backyard, making a huge spectacle of himself as he tried once more to make people think that *I* was the one who had the problems. I was relieved when he disappeared into a neighbor's empty trailer home. What a disappointment it was to see through the window that he sat inside, smoking a glass pipe of meth.

By this time, Naomi was about six months old. In the days following my first concentrated effort to kick Viper out of the house, he barged in twice. Both times he grabbed the baby and ran out the door! When I recovered her the second time, I took her into the boys' bedroom and lifted her up. "Lord, I have dedicated my daughter to you. You have blessed me with the desires of my heart. I love You and commit my daughter to You. And if the devil should try to take my daughter, I will still serve You. God, I pray no weapon formed against my daughter will prosper. Greater are You who are in me than the Devil who comes to kill, steal, and destroy. In Jesus's name, Amen."

Two years from the date when we were first married, I told Viper I wanted a divorce. Two months later, he went to prison.

While the next few months were a struggle since Thomas raised our rent and I knew it would take a while for my housing application to go through so we could find a new place, I tried to focus on my babies and to faithfully minister to others as the Lord brought me opportunity. Little did I know that as I lived according to His Word and sought to be an encouragement, I would be blessed in return!

The first thing I did, at the Lord's prompting, was to open my home and heart to other single moms who needed a break and a little encouragement. The first woman who stayed with me for a week suffered with seizures. Soon after she moved, I came across a woman named Dorcas and her little girl, Rosalynn. She also had a baby boy, and I witnessed to her about Christ as she struggled to figure out what to do about the rough marriage she'd left behind in South Dakota. Shortly thereafter, I began ministering to a woman named Crystal, who had three children: a Caucasian girl and boy and an African American baby girl. In each instance, I gave what I could to pour out on others the same love the Father had showered on me.

All my children were such a gift to me, but Naomi—who had none of her biological dad's negative characteristics—was the smile of my day. I was so proud of her, and I enjoyed every moment I could spend with her and her siblings. Just before Naomi's first birthday, I received my housing approval. For the first time in years, my children and I were able to move without the snake chasing our heels. No longer codependent, I was free. However, gaining my boys' trust and respect would not be easily accomplished.

13

Let's Pack, We're Moving

You will keep him in perfect peace, whose mind is
stayed on You, because he trusts in You.

—Isaiah 26:3

As soon as I received my housing approval, I began looking
for a place to live. I knew what I wanted in a new home,
and I did not want to stay in Salttown City anymore. I
prayed about moving to the city of Laidback. I asked the
Lord to please help me locate a clean apartment close to
schools, shopping, doctors' offices, and a city bus stop. I also
requested that the place be big enough to accommodate my
California king-size bed.

My search got off to a poor start as I opened the doors
to a couple of places that were small and run down—not to
mention cockroach invested. My frustration mounted when
I saw some beautiful townhomes in nearby Farmington,
knowing at a glance they were absolutely too expensive. But

in the end, God led me to the perfect home in Layton: my Father provided for all my desires, and the price was right.

The children liked our new place, and I was happy, free, and independent. What a relief it was to know that Viper would be in prison until November of 1995! As soon as the kids and I were settled, I sought a legal aid attorney to secure full custody of Naomi before his release. Viper had already refused to accept our divorce papers. I knew he'd fight even harder against the matter of custody.

On Sundays, either Grace or Stan would pick us up, take us to church, and then deliver us home. Saint John provided us with a VCR to go along with the television Viper had reintroduced into our lives. Saint John taped many Christian videos for me, including the life of Jesus cartoons, *Quigley's Village*, episodes of Christy, *Little House on the Prairie*, and music videos by Carman.

I was also able to better disciple my kids in their knowledge of the Lord because of a set of children's Bible story books that included lessons appropriate for two different age groups. The children loved that, and I read to them and prayed with them often.

No longer burdened by Viper's constant interference, I was able to get involved in what they were doing in school, to oversee their friendships, and to make sure we celebrated holidays such as the Easter Resurrection and Christmas in a way that was honoring to the Lord. And in a move that was probably even more important than anything else

I accomplished in those days, I began holding a morning quiet time in my room each day. The whole family knew that Mom was talking to the Lord during that time, and the children knew not to bother me unless it was extremely important.

God honored my renewed commitment to my faith and my efforts to serve Him. As time went on, I accumulated furniture by way of others throwing it out or selling it, and before long, I had a kitchen table and chairs, two sets of bunk beds, and eventually a washer and dryer. The children were happier than I'd ever seen them, and I was immensely relieved that I could finally offer them an abuse-free environment. Though life as a single parent was not easy, I found myself feeling so blessed one day as I was pushing a shopping cart home from the store in the snow that happy tears ran down my face. God was so faithful to care for me!

The children and I lived in that apartment for five years. When we first moved in, Rani—who still lived with her aunt—was ten and in the fifth grade. Bren Ashton was nine and in the fourth grade. Ethan, age five, was in the first grade. Daniel was two, and Naomi had just turned a year old.

Ethan, Jared's son, most challenged my parenting skills in those days. Guessing that the little guy was missing having a father figure in his life, I began to write to Jared, who was in prison. Jared wrote back with a surprising amount of compassion and understanding for our little boy.

After having Jeb speak with him on the phone, I got Ethan into counseling and had him tested in school. It turned out he had an above average IQ score. He was incredibly intelligent, and I knew he needed challenge and a chance to succeed. I soon found that as long as Ethan was committed to doing something constructive, he was not disruptive. Even as a child, he was good-looking, charming, and smart enough to pull the wool over just about anybody. Even his teachers found it difficult to keep him on task. I kept taking him to the Lord in prayer, asking for guidance and requesting that God keep his heart soft.

There were days when Ethan and Bren reminded me of Cain and Abel. Bren, though bright and handsome, hated Ethan, who everyone seemed to think was clever and cute. Though Bren's teacher thought him intelligent enough to skip not just one but two grades, he continued to struggle with bringing home important papers from school, and he sometimes allowed his anger to control his behavior when things didn't go the way he wanted. It was so difficult for me the day my baby announced he was going to live with Brett and his stepmother.

Trying to respect my boy's need for a father figure, I let him go. Sadly, I had no idea that his dad was using and would allow our twelve-year-old son to hang out with kids involved in a gang. I was shocked when Bren returned home unexpectedly—a troubled, very angry version of the boy who had left. I did not discover the source of his emotion until much later: my sweet son was left to conquer the haunting memories of living through a drive-by shooting at his dad's house. His friend was shot and had died in his lap! My compassionate, compliant, and helpful son was never quite the same after that.

Meanwhile, Daniel—son of Dudley—grew increasingly stubborn and began stealing. His biological father would come to see him on occasion, and I noticed how quiet and observant Daniel was in those interactions. For the most part, in fact, Daniel was stubbornly set against speaking. Hoping to help him find his way and to help him also overcome a stutter, I enrolled him in speech therapy. He finally let go of his refusal to talk when they brought in a pretty new therapist. I could see he was improving, and I worked to honor his desire that I make complete eye contact with him in all our interactions. Still, one day, he said he wanted to run away. I teasingly told him he could if he could first learn to tie his shoes all by himself. That brought a smile.

In this particular season of our lives, not a day went by that I didn't talk to the Lord about my little family. Every chance I got, I tried to help fill the gaps left by my children's biological fathers with the love of their Heavenly Father. On Wednesdays, though we were tired from work and school, I'd pack a paper-sack dinner for each of us, and we would head to the bus stop. Three separate bus rides later, we would arrive at church.

More than anything else, I wanted to instill in my growing children the assurance of Psalm 27:10: "When my father...forsake[s] me, Then the Lord will take care of me."

14

Take Heed, Be Cautious and Alert

Be sober, be vigilant; because your adversary the
devil walks about like a roaring lion, seeking whom
he may devour.

—1 Peter 5:8

IN 1994, I finally received temporary, notarized custody
of Rani. For many years, I had longed for the day when
my girl would be safe under my roof. Her arrival was the
answer to many prayers, and I hoped that it would spell the
end of the general neglect and abuse she'd endured until
then. By the day she moved her things into our home, my
firstborn was in the fifth grade. Though not yet thirteen,
Rani was a bit wild and promiscuous. It made me so sad to
see those traits in her; I desperately wanted my baby not to
repeat my mistakes!

At first, I overlooked a lot of her misbehavior, wanting
so much to help her through the most difficult stages of her

life. I knew from experience that going from child to tween to teen to adult is not an easy process. Further, the choices she would have to face in those soon-to-arrive years had the potential to mark her life forever. I wanted to help her avoid trouble, and I hoped she would gain as much from ongoing church involvement as I had. I remember that she would lay her head on my lap in church, and I would run my fingers through her hair. Those times were so precious to me.

For a while, things went well. Rani was a wonderful help: she was gifted at keeping the house and watching her siblings. Our greatest tension was her rebellious mouth, but I understood why she struggled with that. She was accustomed to having to defend her every action. Sadly, one day, Rani and I got into an argument. It was the only one we'd had, but it was a biggie. In retrospect, I realize that had I given my anger over to the Lord that afternoon rather than allowing it to build, I could have saved us a whole lot of heartache. Instead, I gave the devil a foothold in my heart. That anger became a crack in my spiritual armor, and he was ready to exploit it.

Behind the argument was the fact that Rani had been caught sneaking out of her room midday and shoplifting a pair of sunglasses. The whole situation had rattled me so completely that I made a hasty call to her Aunt Mara. In a move I would deeply regret soon after I hung up the phone, I mentioned that Rani might benefit from a stay in a Christian girls' home. The Home of the Good Shepherd had, after all, done me some good. But why I voiced such a thought to the very woman who had stolen my daughter from me years before is beyond my comprehension.

That evening, I went to work at Shopko, across the street from our apartment. Rani was watching Jake and Naomi for me, and I was surprised when I received a call from her. My business didn't smile on us taking personal calls.

"Mom," Rani said in a panic, "Aunt Mara is here to take me! She'd brought the police with her."

Feeling my heart constrict, I asked a coworker to take over my register and then ran to the apartment as fast as I could. By that time, Rani was in tears and rightly ready to blame me for this unexpected turn of events as she headed out the door with her aunt. Her last words to me sank deeply into my spirit: "I told you not to call my aunt, Mom!" I felt like such a failure—I had so thoroughly let us both down. It didn't help that Naomi and Daniel were left without a sitter, but that fact, which would certainly complicate our lives, seemed minor compared with the heartbreak of knowing how deeply I had disappointed Rani and reinforced her aunt's belief that I failed as the child's mother.

Knowing I could not get back to work until I covered the childcare situation, I called Shopko and tried to explain my hasty departure. The next day, however, I still received a major chewing out and was told that nothing could come before my job. "If you do not like following our orders and procedures," my boss said, "then you can just leave." Tears ran down my face at those words because I did not want to lose my job, but I had to put my children first. "I will have to quit," I said.

In time, I was able to secure other childcare, and I got a job at Sconecutter. It was a fast-food restaurant that specialized in baking scones. I prepared food, made fries, took and filled the orders, and created yummy frozen yogurt shakes. In addition, I kept the tables cleaned off, vacuumed the store, mopped the floors, and did the dishes. I was sad when the place closed down after being open for only a year.

My next place of employment was Hill Air Force Base. I received this opportunity through my interactions with PARC (Pioneering Adult Rehab Center), a place that helped me cope with my ADHD disability. I worked as a janitor in a building where I was constantly amazed to find that adults wrote on the bathroom stalls and neglected to flush the toilets. Even more alarming was the fact that a couple of the other janitors thought nothing of using the same cleaning rags on the sinks that they had just used to wipe down the toilets! (Those folks I reported immediately.)

My main coworker's name was Mel. She and I would walk to the eight different buildings together, lift heavy mop buckets, and push carts around the campus. Sometimes we went to the base thrift store together when our shift ended or when we were caught up with the day's work. We would browse the aisles, and I loved to buy Ethan jet models because he confessed he wanted to fly for the air force one day. I even found a black panther that purred and bought it for my own kitten, Naomi. Overall, I made a lot of good memories in that place where I worked for two years. That was the longest I had ever held a job.

I was eventually moved to a more secure building that could be entered only with a security card. This place housed a computer room as well as a few other confidential and top secret places I can't mention. I quickly found that I liked it there; it was nice to clean only the one building all day. In time, however, my back began to suffer from years of poor lifting practices. The day came when I knew my pain was a problem that had to be addressed. I ended up claiming worker's compensation and going to physical therapy.

In those days while I rested my back, I enjoyed the time I could spend with my kids. We continued to watch Christian videos together, and I loved to hear Ethan sing along with Carman. That boy sang "Satan Bite the Dust" with so much passion that it brought tears to my eyes. Another family video, a recording of the dramatic production *Heaven's Gates and Hell's Flames*, was Naomi's favorite. She'd watch that Easter drama and say, "That's Jesus, huh, Momma, huh?" As tiny as she was, she wanted to understand the story of Jesus and the eternal life He offers those who love Him.

Daniel never said much about the steady stream of faith-based shows we watched, but I noticed he did carefully observe them. It broke my heart, though, to realize my precious Rani wasn't there to join us. Though she would come back occasionally in the coming months, I felt I had failed her.

One day as I was thinking about how much it hurt that I could not be a consistent, daily part of Rani's life, it occurred to me how sad it was that Viper could not be a part of Naomi's. Though I was actively seeking a divorce from him and still feared his cruel abuse toward me, I—in a moment of weakness—wrote to him in prison. I foolishly let him know where we lived.

About this same time, I went to Outfield High School with a couple of the kids in town and finally obtained my certificate of completion for drivers' training. I used a friend's Pontiac Grand Am to take my driving test, and I passed!

When I was able to return to work, I began to talk to a jet engine mechanic named Nelson. The man was a total hippie. He had long hair and a floppy walking stride. Nelson was a quiet bachelor, and he liked me. Whether it happened because I was attracted to him, because I was lonesome, or simply because I was tired of parenting on my own, I soon began to date him.

On the plus side, Nelson owned a home, an old red truck, a Jet Ski, and a silver sports car; he made good money. A few negatives that I was far too quick to overlook included the facts that he had a son he didn't bother to locate, made no secret that he cheated on drug tests by substituting urine that was not his own, and smoked pot while watching crass cartoons. Every one of those things sent the alarm bells in my head into a deafening chorus of "Stay away from that guy!" Sadly, I failed to listen to the warning.

In the beginning of our relationship, things were platonic between us. I told myself it was okay that my friend had no relationship with God—maybe he would come to know Him through my witness. Yet even when our brief conversations failed to take the helpful spiritual turn I had initially hoped they would, I continued to justify our get-togethers by telling myself we were just hanging out as friends.

While at first we went out to eat and made a few trips to the movies together, a little later Nelson met my children. He would come over to visit occasionally, and he even bought us a kitten named Dins-dale. Ethan, who was forever bringing home strays, took to the little cat right away and gave Prince, a Siamese, to Nelson in return. After that, things started to progress quickly. It wasn't long before an old temptation came knocking.

Nelson invited me to a sleepover at his house, and I knew he was not interested in sitting up to tell ghost stories and bake cookies. The Holy Spirit warned me strongly that I should not go to Nelson's that night; instead, I was to run from that relationship and not look back. But by that time,

I'd allowed the lust in my heart to grow. I missed intimacy. I craved companionship. Once again I began to believe that things in my life would go more smoothly if I could just find the right man. And so, I ignored the fact that I was still married to Viper.

I ignored the fact that I belonged to a God firmly against sex outside the marriage relationship. I went to bed with my boyfriend that night. And the truth is that I neither loved Nelson nor saw him as a prospect for marriage. As so many women before me have done, I allowed my loneliness and need to drive me into an intimate relationship. (It is easy to fall in this trap and hard to get out. It also hurts that person who may have strong feelings for you even if your feelings are not the same. It is wrong to use people for the benefits. Yes, even if they are all you have.)

Perhaps even more terrible than the choice I made to sleep with Nelson was the fact that I left the kids alone for the evening so I could feed my desires. At first that seemed like a good idea since capable Rani was staying with me for a few days, and I knew she could keep charge for a while. But throughout the evening, I kept feeling sick with worry—or maybe guilt. I kept calling my children that evening, once on the hour until it was too late for them to still be awake. I tried to make myself feel better by remembering I had ordered them dinner and had rented them movies to watch before I left. The five had strict orders not to answer the door unless it was me.

However, I had not bargained on the fact that several of my babies were old enough to recognize that what I was doing was not only wrong but was in direct violation of the kind of life.

I taught them to live. My children came to see me as a hypocrite, and what started as one act of sexual sin forever compromised my relationship with my kids and brought more trouble than I could have imagined.

15

Unraveling

> Giving all diligence, add to your faith virtue,
> to virtue knowledge, to knowledge self-control,
> to self-control perseverance, to perseverance
> godliness, to godliness brotherly kindness,
> and to brotherly kindness love. For if these things
> are yours and abound, you will be neither barren
> nor unfruitful in the knowledge of our Lord Jesus
> Christ.
>
> —2 Peter 1:3–8

It's easy for people to judge one another harshly, to zero in on one another's failures without attempting to extend the same measure of grace that Father God provides. The hardest part of sharing my story is allowing the ugly things of my life to surface. To highlight my failures and to admit to the times when I neglected to live up to the virtues associated with the faith I claim.

I don't tell about this difficult period of my life lightly, but I do share it with a purpose. I want others to know what it took me many years to figure out: the choices we make today are going to affect others tomorrow, and no matter how desperately we might wish to do so, we cannot fix yesterday.

Not for a moment do I regret having any of my children. However, I do regret that I did not give them a stable home. And to this day, I grieve that my sinful choices brought them abuse, neglect, and insecurity. How I wish my younger self had known the value of thinking before I acted. I owed it to my babies to act responsibly. I was the beginning link in the chain of events that would shape the worldviews and choices that Rani, Bren, Ethan, Daniel, and Naomi would make.

Today, I am more mature in my walk with Christ and recognize that each person will be held accountable for the things he or she did or did not do, for the things he or she said or did not say (see Rev. 20:11–15). I know that God's Word says, "To him who knows to do good and does not do *it*, to him it is sin" (James 4:17). But in the early days of my faith journey, in those years when my children were young and the cost of my choices was high, I continually fell back on the knowledge that God's mercy endures forever. As far too many of us do, I treated His grace and mercy lightly— sometimes taking it for granted altogether.

The forgiveness Christ offers is not a license to sin. I hate that I allowed my children to witness otherwise. (Needing someone because he or she is helping you out versus obeying the Father or obeying the law is a difficult choice. I know it is far better to trust God than put your trust in people. In addition, to what they do for you.) In the days of my relationship with Nelson, I did try to keep up with church and to continue to make the Christian faith a part of my kids' lives.

God was faithful to bless my family. I recall that about the time Nelson and I started seeing each other, a sub for Santa program stepped in to provide the kids and me with a great Christmas. The boys received bikes, and Naomi got a play kitchen. They also gave us food and a card. Inside were ten one-hundred-dollar bills. Never in my life had I held so much money in my hand! I immediately tithed on the blessing and used the remainder to buy practical things we needed.

Meanwhile, Ronan and Grace did their best to discourage me from continuing in my romantic involvement. Grace gently reminded me of what my attorney had already made clear: Viper had still not signed our divorce papers, and the warden had ignored my pleas for help in securing sole custody of Naomi. She cautioned me with 1 Corinthians 6:9–10: "Do you not know that the unrighteous will not inherit the kingdom of God? Do not be deceived. Neither fornicators, nor idolaters, nor adulterers…will inherit the kingdom of God." Also in her loving arsenal of Scripture was Galatians 6:7: "Do not be deceived, God is not mocked; for whatever a man sows, that he will also reap." Sadly, I didn't allow her reminders to lead to a breakup with my boyfriend though I did speak to Nelson about my desire to abstain from sexual intimacy.

I am thankful that neither Ronan nor Grace gave up on me. They even bought me a used car—which turned out to be a complete lemon, though the thought behind their gift was nice. And Ronan continued to encourage me to get up early each day to pray over my children. (Was a warning and urgency request.)

Before 1996 dawned, the thing I'd long dreaded came to pass. Viper was released from prison, and he went to live in a halfway house where he would remain while on probation. Armed with the address I'd sent him in a moment of nostalgia, he came to see three-year-old Naomi. He asked her if she wanted to come stay at his house. The very idea struck fear in my heart. I told him she was not leaving with him unless he first granted me full custody. After that, he'd have to get to know her slowly as I supervised before I'd be willing to let her visit with him.

He left energetically, obviously determined to make sure I did not get custody. His first stop was Dudley's house. He tried to bribe my son Daniel's dad with money, encouraging him to tell the DHS workers that I was an unfit and abusive mother. Thankfully, Dudley refused to do such a thing. He knew I loved my children, and they loved me.

My dad still lived in Missouri when Viper walked back into my life, and he didn't like the idea of the just-released-from-prison man running off with my child any more than I did. Dad told me to sell all I had and move to Missouri. But as I remembered the challenges that came with trying to move in with him before, I knew his offer would never work out. Further, I remembered the anti-African American sentiments that some in Missouri still held. I would not expose my Naomi to their prejudice.

Ronan and Grace discouraged the Missouri idea too. Their response to the situation was to pray for me and encourage me to keep getting up at four in the morning to pray for guidance. I did try to follow their advice, forcing myself out of bed before daylight so I could spend time speaking with God. But Naomi invariably followed me to the couch for this quiet time, and it was so difficult to pray without falling asleep!

In retrospect, I'm reminded of the Bible story about Jesus asking the disciples to pray with Him as the hour of His crucifixion approached (see Matt. 26). Numerous times those men fell asleep on this job until He finally asked, "Could you not watch with Me one hour?" Unfortunately, I found it hard to stand on guard for Christ too.

Meanwhile, things were increasingly difficult where my sons were concerned. Bren continued to struggle with all he had experienced at his dad's house. His mood swings were made more difficult by the fact that Brutus and his wife had put the boy in a karate class for a short time. When Bren came home to me, he was very anxious to use his karate skills on his mother anytime we didn't see eye to eye.

Ethan, who still managed to bring out the worst in his older brother, was forever testing and pushing my buttons through misbehavior at home and at school. He refused to stay in time-out and laughed, screamed, and yelled at me when I attempted to spank him. As both boys chafed against authority and began to match me in strength and size, I found it almost impossible to discipline them. Add to this Daniel's increasing stubbornness about changing his clothes, his love of writing on the walls with a marker, and his overdose on children's chewable vitamins and it's easy to see I had my hands full.

I enrolled Ethan in a program called KYTE, which was geared toward counseling and helping low-income families with troubled children. Each Wednesday night, I'd eat dinner with other families whose kids were a part of the program, and then the gathering would break into smaller groups. I trusted the lead therapist there, and I hoped that those in my support group might be able to suggest some ways to help my boys.

I briefly shared about my struggles with Bren, who by this time was always trying to intimidate me and was growing increasingly physical toward me. (By this time, Bren was in the Quest Program and had been put on probation for using aggression and threats.) A counselor named Miss Hardy and a couple of social workers who were present didn't seem the least bit interested in helping me get my boys under control. "There isn't anything we can do to help you at this point," I was told. "We cannot take the two boys into state's custody if that is what you're asking us to do." I frowned. I didn't want the boys in anyone's custody but my own, but I did need support in getting some order and discipline in our home!

Was there not a youth facility that could step in to help reinforce respect and to help my kids learn to listen to me?

Eventually, I reached out to an organization that worked with Family Services and Mental Health in Laidback City. They tried to address my concerns by providing us with some in-home therapy. The mentor they sent was a man named John. I soon found that his form of intervention left my home in more chaos than ever before. Everything he told me to do seemed to have a backward effect. Only Naomi, ball of energy and laughter that she was, brought me joy during this difficult time. The lyrics of a song from 1989 always make me think of her:

> When I see you smile
> Sometimes I wonder
> How I'd ever make it through,
> Through this world without having you
> I just wouldn't have a clue

For the first several months of 1995, I poured myself into work, volunteering at the schools, attending counseling sessions, and doing all I could to keep the kids content and entertained. As the weather warmed, I made a point to play outside with the children, often heading down to the pool with them. I loved them so much, and the importance of my involvement with D paled in comparison with my relationships with them. My connection with my Father, however, had begun to unravel.

One night, the director of the KYTE program called me into her office. Ethan, she reported, had been telling everyone that I planned to send him to a foster home. While this was untrue, the KYTE staff felt it was worth investigating. They sent a woman from DHS to check our home and my parenting. We both received her approval. Ethan got a scolding for making up lies to gain attention.

Not long after that day, Bren wanted to go bowling with his friend. We had a lot of things on the calendar that week, and I told him no. He was upset with my decision and physically attacked me over it. Fearful he would hurt one or both of us, I managed to grab his twelve-year-old shoulders and seat him firmly on a stool by the door. I used my weight to brace him against the wall and gave him a warning that had been a long time coming: "Bren, if you are going to act like a violent, grown man, I will protect myself as if you are. This stuff stops, or I will knee you in the groin."

Ethan, who was usually at odds with his brother, chose to join in the fight against Mom. "I'm going with him to that bowling alley!" he yelled defiantly, probably hoping to give his brother new fighting resolve in the face of my threat.

"No, you're not," I said, turning to him. "Shut up that talk right now!"

The eight-year-old didn't hush. He cursed me.

Immediately, I decided I'd had enough of being bullied by my own children. Without thinking, I slapped him in the mouth. Out popped his front tooth, which had been hanging by a thread for the last several days. Ethan grabbed his mouth and went hysterical. As his voice rose and I kicked at him in a futile attempt to stop the insanity, I knew I'd officially lost control of our home.

The following Wednesday, Ethan attended the KYTE program as usual. On that particular day, his class was asked to draw pictures showing what happened when their parents got angry. Ethan, of course, illustrated the tooth incident that was still fresh in his mind. Things got worse when he explained the story behind it.

Later in group therapy, I was handed the picture Ethan drew. I was devastated by what was depicted on that paper, knowing no one would believe that his account showed only a moment in our home life and completely neglected the fact that I dearly loved and tried to be patient with my children on most occasions.

I felt so humiliated, realizing from the look in Counselor Hardy's eyes that she believed only the worst about me. I tried to apologize for my momentary loss of control. I explained that Ethan's latest behavior—modifying medication had been contributing to his aggressiveness and that I wanted him off it. But no one cared what I had to say. Their judgment fell like an anvil on my heart. (I did not know at this time that Ethan had lied to Hardy about Naomi being spanked.)

A week later, on March 15, 1996, I clocked out at work and picked Naomi up from day care. Just as I started dinner, the boys came home from school and went out to play. While I waited for the Hamburger Helper to cook, Naomi and I curled together in the recliner. Watching *The Miracles of Jesus* with my little kitten was the highlight of my day. It would have been nice to sit there with her for hours, but I knew it was time to call the boys inside.

I scooped my little one off my lap and set her back in the chair. But just as I turned to walk into the kitchen, a heavy knock on the door made my heart skip a beat. *Viper?*

Trembling, I looked out the peephole to see whether my fears were justified. On the porch stood the social worker who had previously approved my home and parenting as well as three Layton police officers. And unlike Viper, who wanted nothing more than to take my sweet Naomi, I'd soon learn that this group planned to take all my children from me. Rani, Bren, Ethan, Daniel, and Naomi were all in danger of becoming wards of the state. That which I had greatly feared had come upon me. The course of our lives was about to change forever.

"So," the devil, that ancient enemy hissed in my mind as the group on my porch made its way into my home, "where is your 'Heavenly Father' now? Will you still serve Him when all you hold dear is gone?"

A single tear slipped down my cheek.

Though I knew the Bible would tell me God was as near to me as ever, I wasn't certain how to answer that last question. Could I still serve the Lord when I'd messed up so royally? Would I still serve Him when life became a sea of new hurts?

Only time would tell.

Epilogue

Rani, now an adult and mother of seven, read the last chapter of my story and warned me that no one likes a sad ending. "Mom, people hate it when movies end like that!"

I took her concern to heart, but I knew I couldn't change it. *Because You Loved Me and Never Let Go: A Father's Love for His Daughter* is one of three books that tell the story of my life. While the Lord continued to work out His plans for me over the years between the last page of my first book and those I've yet to publish, I don't want to give everything away in the first installment.

Still, I can appreciate that no one likes a sad close, so I want to end on a happy note.

My dad, the Dutch Irishman originally from California, gave his heart to the Lord around the same time Rani was born. Not long after that, he was delivered from his addictions to alcohol and cigarettes. In the events recounted in this story, Dad and his wife—much like myself—were not perfect followers of the walk they claim; however, I hope people will extend them grace as every Christian is a work in progress. Today, my dad publically teaches against many religious occults and has brought many to the light of Jesus through his testimony. We have a growing relationship on FB. I don't hesitate to do whatever is in my means to so, because I love him unconditionally.

To this day, Dad and his wife, live in Missouri.

My mother, Sharon Rose, has come through a lot of change since the days of bitterness and cruelty shared early in my story. Her coming to accept Jesus Christ as her Lord and Savior in 1990 was a beautiful miracle. Mom's relationship with the Father has worked to keep us loving each other and forgiving our past failures. With the love, peace, and forgiveness of Almighty God the Father and His Holy Spirit working in her, Mom has found freedom from her wrongs.

She loves the truth of Proverbs 4:22: "[God's words] are life to those who find them, and health to all their flesh." When once she walked in a body crippled by bitterness and poor choices, she now walks each day in the freedom and grace of the Lord.

In the years since her salvation, Mom has been a huge blessing to me. She loves to give to others and has faithfully prayed for her children, grandchildren, and great-grandkids throughout the years. Even today, when I need someone to pray with me, she is there. She always answers the phone with "Praise the Lord." I phone her often.

When I need to get things off my chest, she listens with compassion and understanding. What a blessing it is to see Mom—a woman once so lost—now actively loving the Lord with all her heart, mind, and soul. Her inward beauty far outshines the physical beauty of her younger days, and I am now happy to call her my friend.

For Mom:

Despite all flaws of times past,
I come to realize that her days are ending quite fast.
Oh, how my thoughts wonder
Of making her days last longer.
Her laughter and her smile will bring each of us
Health and strength with joys and fond memories
That will last a long while.
The West can be so cold and dreary,
So she chooses to stay in bed with her aches and pains,
Her bones get tired and weary.
If only I could but cherish each moment of our time,
Having tea and conversation, just knowing I gave her my best and my all
Before our Father comes to call my mother and my friend.
I know she understands her prayers avail much.
Whom will I turn to when you are gone?
For I'm now the mother my daughters lean on and come to call.
I will surely be here.

For each fall that brings a tear and a heart full of
pain in sunshine and rain
On my feeble knees, I will pray for my family to
join me
That glorious day when my Lord comes to carry
me home.
Thanks to all those who
Lead the way
For many of us without parents to lean on.
The Father is waiting
for you to call.

God takes us as we are, but He loves us enough not to
allow us to stay that way. God will finish the work He
begins in each of His children. How beautiful to watch
those transformations take place—even when they don't
happen overnight.

"The will of God will never take you where the grace of
God will not protect you."

I pray that you would know that God has great plans
instore for you life.

He is a wonderful loving father and he has an amazing
future for you.

May you trust in His plans no matter how things look
right now.

Life is hard, but God provides,
Life is unpredictable, but God guides
Life is unfair, but God cares,
Life is always a challenge,
But God sustains.

There is 1 cross
1 Savior, 1 written word of God
He is the only truth
The only way and life
Come follow Him while He can still be found.

Watch your thoughts
They become your words
Watch your words
They become your Actions
Watch your actions
They become your habits
Watch your habits
They become your character
Watch your character it becomes your Destiny.

Author's Note

THERE IS THEREFORE now no condemnation to those who are in Christ Jesus, who do not walk according to the flesh but according to the Spirit (Rom. 8:1).

John 8:1–11 tells the story of a woman caught in the act of adultery just before being thrown at the feet of Jesus. Her accusers hoped to stone her to death. Perhaps they thought Jesus would join them. But He didn't. Instead, He saved her from a terrible fate by making an interesting statement: "He who is without sin among you, let him throw a stone at her first." No one, according to Jesus, is without sin. Without His perfect love and forgiveness, every one of us deserves death (see Rom. 6:23).

Each time I read this passage, I'm aware that I was an adulterer, fornicator, thief, liar, and a manipulator. The world said of me, "She is worthless, dumb, rebellious, an adulterer, and a harlot!" But rather than sentencing me to an eternity without God and a life without hope, Jesus showed me mercy. He lifted my chin, looked into my eyes with compassion, and said softly, "Believe in Me and repent. Your sins are forgiven."

Maybe you have been an outcast or have been judged for where you live, for collecting government assistance, for living in a foster home, or because you've spent time in prison. Perhaps you feel like you wear a sign on your back that says one of the following: Poor. Stupid. Criminal. Felon. Divorced. Single parent. Orphan. In any case, know that the God who created you does not brand you with such names or discount you because of your past or because of something in your present.

John 3:16 assures us that "God so loved the world that He gave His only begotten Son, that whoever believes in Him should not perish but have everlasting life." That means God the Father loves *you* so much that He decided to pay the penalty for your wrongs. He sent His Son, Jesus, to die on the cross as a sacrifice for all your sins. Jesus saw all you've ever done but took stripes, persecution, and the crucifixion just so you could one day live with Him in heaven! (See John 17:24.) You can be forgiven. You can be free!

The world is full of religions like Mormonism that give people a list of rules and traditions to follow in the hope of somehow connecting to God. Only in Christianity does God reach out to humanity, offering forgiveness and hope to all who will simply accept that His Son died in their place. He gave His life so we could become righteous in Him (see 2 Cor. 5:21).

Romans 5:8 says, "God demonstrates His own love toward us, in that while we were still sinners, Christ died for us." This means we don't have to clean ourselves up before we come to Jesus. He knows all about our ugly actions, and He loves us anyway.

Like a potter reshaping a clay pot that seems damaged beyond repair, so He is the master potter who longs to reshape and correct the clay of our hearts. Romans 10:9–10 builds on the knowledge that we are all sinners and tells us how to find forgiveness and to accept God as our Father: "If you confess with your mouth the Lord Jesus and believe in your heart that God has raised Him from the dead, you will be saved. For with the heart one believes unto righteousness, and with the mouth confession is made unto salvation." Romans 5:1 ties it all together: "Having been justified by faith (that is, having been made just as if we never sinned), we have peace with God through our Lord Jesus Christ."

My Father wants to be your Father; He will never leave you or give up on you. His love is unconditional. He created you and has a purpose and destiny laid out for you if only you'll invite Him into your life. "'Come to Me, all *you* who labor and are heavy laden,' He says, 'and I will give you rest'" (see Matt. 11:28).

It is my prayer that you will come to know the Lord who has made such radical changes in me—many of them long after the season this book recounts.

May you live in the knowledge that with Jesus you are not alone! You are beautiful! And better days are ahead.

Appendix A

Songs and Poems

Jesus Culture, "One Thing Remains," by Chris Quilala, Come Away. 2012 by Bethel Music.

Randall, Naomi W., "I Am a Child of God," *Sing with Me: Songs for Children.* Salt Lake: Deseret Book Company, 1969.

Bad English, "When I See You Smile." 1989 by Epic Records.

Author Unknown. "He Leads the Way." Posted October 4, 2012. http://callongod.org/poems.htm. Accessed April 4, 2013.

Ken Ham, "Are There Really Different Races?" Posted November 29, 2007. http://www.answersingenesis.org/articles/nab/are-there-different-races. Accessed April 4, 2013.

GOD WANTS YOU to know how special you are to Him. No matter what you're going through, others have been through it too. Multiple organizations and ministries can help provide you with basic needs as you seek the direction of the Father. See the suggestions in the back of this book.

For information on ministries available to those who need support in overcoming addiction or abuse, please see the "Helpful Resources" list at the back of this book.

Over the years, I've learned that true discipline is meant not to punish but to teach. Rather than reacting to our kids' misbehavior in anger, we should remember that the Lord disciplines His kids with love. Love, not anger or revenge, must be the engine behind discipline.

Compromising one's values always leads to regrets!

Parenting is not easy, but it is worth it! A lifetime of observation has taught me that when a single parent commits to bringing up his or her children according to God's Word, he or she will see many blessings. Even better, the children will grow into adults who respect that Mom or Dad endured hardships and pressed on.

If you are parenting alone, please keep Matthew 26:41 in mind: "Watch and pray, lest you enter into temptation. The spirit indeed *is* willing, but the flesh *is* weak."

Appendix B

Helpful Resources

GOD WANTS TO heal you emotionally, physically, spiritually, and mentally. He wants to deliver you from any addictions, anger, or issues. He wants to free you of abuse, condemnation, and disappointments. There is no problem too great for God.

The first step is simply to ask Jesus for forgiveness, to believe that He is the Son of God who died and rose again to pay the cost for your sins. The next step is to begin reading God's Word, the Bible, and to start attending a church where the authority of His Word is taught. Helpful too is immersing yourself in other resources that will enrich your understanding of the Lord and will help you focus your life around Him.

For practical assistance, contact your local, Bible-believing church. Briefly share your story and humbly ask for what you need.

204 | Shamara Rainforest

Seek financial guidance: *www.myfinancialprograms.com/*

Obtain legal assistance: *www:/requestlegalhelp.org*

Find help in overcoming addiction: Ocean Breeze Recovery or Teen Challenge Seek housing and support to help you escape abuse: *http://www.williamsabellfoundation. org/support_abused_women_and_children*

Apply for a grant to help you start over after surviving abuse: *http://www.webofbenefit.org/*

Obtain caring support to cope with a surprise pregnancy: *http://www.priestsforlife.org/pregnant-need-help/index.aspx*

For marriage and family help, visit helpguide.org, a nonprofit organization dedicated to providing mental health information you can trust.

Read Dr. Emerson Eggerichs' book, *Love and Respect* (Nashville: Thomas Nelson, 2004) to find new hope for your marriage.

Discover the parenting and marriage geared teachings of Dr. James Dobson: *www.focusonthefamily.com.*

A marriage built on God's foundation will not be destroyed during the storms for spiritual growth. Bevere, John. *Driven by Eternity.* Nashville: FaithWords, 2006.

Copeland, Gloria. *Walk with God.* Fort Worth, TX: Kenneth Copeland Ministries, 1996.

Dickow, Gregory. *From the Inside Out: A Revolutionary 40-Day Fast from Wrong Thinking.* Flowood, MS: Ministry Solutions, 2008.

Lucado, Max. *Experiencing the Heart of Jesus: Knowing His Heart and Feeling His Love.* Nashville: Nelson, 2013.

Experiencing the Words of Jesus: Hearing His Voice and Trusting His Words. Nashville: Thomas Nelson, 2009.

Moore, Beth. *Breaking Free: Discover the Victory of Total Surrender.* Nashville: B&H: 2007.

Thomas, Angela. *Do You Think I'm Beautiful?* Nashville: Thomas Nelson, 2005.

Web sites and businesses geared toward the Christian family:

www.angeltv.org/

www.parables.tv/start-watching-now-registration

www.familytv.com

www.billygraham.org

www. http://lifestylechristianity.com/

www.godvine.com

www.lightsource.com

www.biblestudytools.com

www.cbd.com

www.christianradio.com

www.christianword.org/

http://www.familychristian.com/video/stories-of-faith

www.focusonthefamily.com/

www.crosscards.com

www.kgospeltube.com

www.ibelieve.com

www.jesus.org

www.oneplace.com

www.klove.com/

www.moorelife.org

www.air1.com/

http://www.values4kids.com/

www.worldchallenge.org/about_david_wilkerson

Just to list a few of my favorites. Always make sure what you read or listen to lines up with the Word of God from Genesis to Revelation, nothing added and nothing taken away.

A List of Christian Movies

Check *imbd.com* for ratings and info.

The Grace Card

Facing the Giants

Flywheel

Fireproof

Courageous

Soul Surfer

www.purflix.com

The Encounter 1 and 2

In the Blink of an Eye

The Passion of the Christ

The Bible (2013 TV miniseries)

The Ultimate Gift

Changing Hearts

Cowboys and Angels

Gifted Hands: The Ben Carson Story

Amazing Love (The Story of Hosea)

The Secret Life of Bees

Breaking Free

Rigoletto

Behind the Waterfall

The ButterCream Gang

The Lamp

Akeelah and the Bee

Words by Heart

Rugged Gold

Utopia

The Greening of Whitney Brown

The Blind Side

Important note: When you ask Jesus into your heart and ask Him to forgive you. He sets you free, and whoever the Son sets free is free indeed. Old things are passed away and all things become new. Some of us have more to let go than others.

Start believing what God says about you and don't believe the lies others have told you. You are precious, beautiful, gifted, talented, strong, courageous, giving, lovable and so much more. When you go to this Web site—www.christianword.org/, you can download the prayer book free, and you can order two free books by mail. Word Ministries, 428 Southland Drive, Lexington, Kentucky 40503. If you order more than two books by mail, they ask you to bless the ministry with a $5 per book suggested donation to help cover the cost of publishing and distribution. For more information on ordering, you can call our order informational line at 859-219-9082.

I urge you to get this book and a book for someone else. A bible and this book will help you understand and enlighten your relationship with our Father.

The more I seek your way, the more I want what you desire. I know your everywhere. I know you hear me when I call. You are hope for the hopeless. You are strength for the weak. The chains that bind our troubled hearts and mind with abuse, neglect, and rejection. You see a treasure when others see worthless. You give courage when we are afraid. We are outcasts. You are our Defender and Judge. Our filthy rags you take and replace with your robe of righteousness covered with your blood. You are many names, but to me, You are my Father.